"Haykin has given us a user-friendly introduction to the early centuries of the Christian church. He illustrates the key elements of the church's teaching by referring to the lives and teachings of major figures of the time, most of whom are little known to nonspecialists. Ordinary people need to know about these things, and this book is a great place to begin."

    Gerald Bray, Research Professor of Divinity, Beeson Divinity School

"This gem of a study sparkles with polished clarity. Michael Haykin has skillfully unearthed buried treasures among early church leaders. As an experienced guide, he has drawn from his own personal journey and decades of scholarly research. He presents valuable Patristic insights into apologetic engagement, missional work, spiritual formation, use of Scripture, theological discourse, communal worship, personal piety, and approaches to suffering and martyrdom. From the apostolic fathers to the apostle to Ireland, Haykin's investigations masterfully apply classical wisdom to contemporary concerns."

    Paul Hartog, Associate Professor, Faith Baptist Theological Seminary

"In this introduction, Michael Haykin, an eminent evangelical scholar, opens the door to the riches of early Christianity for evangelicals in a splendidly concise handbook of sorts. Evangelicals, who are experiencing a renaissance of interest in the Fathers, need look no further than this volume for an introduction to many of the most significant figures in Christian history. Readers will be left wanting to learn even more. Evangelicals are indebted to Haykin for this well-written volume."

    Steven A. McKinion, Professor of Theology and Patristics,
    Southeastern Baptist Theological Seminary

Rediscovering
the Church Fathers

Rediscovering

the Church Fathers

WHO THEY WERE
AND HOW THEY SHAPED THE CHURCH

MICHAEL A. G. HAYKIN

WHEATON, ILLINOIS

Rediscovering the Church Fathers: Who They Were and How They Shaped the Church
Copyright © 2011 by Michael A. G. Haykin
Published by Crossway
   1300 Crescent Street
   Wheaton, Illinois 60187

Cover design: Tobias' Outerwear for Books
Cover photo: Bridgeman Art Library
Interior design and typesetting: Lakeside Design Plus
First printing 2011
Printed in the United States of America

Trade paperback ISBN:	978-1-4335-1043-4
PDF ISBN:	978-1-4335-1044-1
Mobipocket ISBN:	978-1-4335-1045-8
ePub ISBN:	978-1-4335-2357-1

Library of Congress Cataloging-in-Publication Data
Haykin, Michael A. G.
  Rediscovering the church fathers : who they were and how they shaped the church / Michael A. G. Haykin.
    p. cm.
  Includes bibliographical references and index.
  ISBN 978-1-4335-1043-4 (tp)
  1. Fathers of the church. 2. Church history—Primitive and early church, ca. 30–600. I. Title.
BR67.H39 2011
270.1—dc22

                   2010045335

Crossway is a publishing ministry of Good News Publishers.

VP		22	21	20	19	18	17	16	15	14	13	12	11
14	13	12	11	10	9	8	7	6	5	4	3	2	1

To

R. Albert Mohler Jr.
Russell D. Moore
Bruce A. Ware
Donald S. Whitney
Gregory A. Wills

—brothers, who, through their various roles of leadership,
have given me the blessed privilege of teaching the church fathers
to fellow Baptists at The Southern Baptist Theological Seminary

CONTENTS

There can be no healthy theology
without a solid grounding in the Fathers.

EDWARD T. OAKES

If I had my time over again, I would have
studied patristics rather than [the] Reformation.

CARL TRUEMAN

Chapter 1

REDISCOVERING THE CHURCH FATHERS

A Vital Need for Evangelicals

Every scribe who has been trained for the kingdom of heaven is like a master of a house, who brings out of his treasure what is new and what is old.

MATTHEW 13:52

A few years after I had completed my doctoral studies in fourth-century pneumatology and exegesis and had started teaching at Central Baptist Seminary in Toronto, I came to realize that I would have to develop another area of scholarly expertise, for very few of the Baptist congregations with which I had contact were keenly interested in men like Athanasius (ca. 299–373) and Basil of Caesarea (ca. 330–379). At a much later date, when I had developed a keen interest in British Baptists and Dissenters in the "long" eighteenth century and was giving papers and lectures in this subject, I was increasingly conscious that while fare from this second area of study was quite acceptable to evangelical audiences, a cloud of suspicion hung over the whole field of the ancient church.

The truth of the matter is that far too many modern-day evangelicals are either ignorant of or quite uncomfortable with the church fathers. No doubt years of their decrying tradition and battling Roman Catholicism and Eastern Orthodoxy with their "saints" from the ancient church have contributed in part to this state of ignorance and unease. Then, too, certain strains of anti-intellectual fundamentalism have discouraged an interest in that "far country" of church history. And the strangeness of much of that era of the ancient church has proven a barrier to some evangelicals in their reading about the early centuries of the church. Finally, an ardent desire to be "people of the Book"—an eminently worthy desire—has also led to a lack of interest in other students of Scripture from that earliest period of the church's history after the apostolic era. Well did Charles Haddon Spurgeon (1834–1892)—a man who certainly could not be accused of elevating tradition to the level of, let alone over, Scripture—once note, "It seems odd, that certain men who talk so much of what the Holy Spirit reveals to themselves, should think so little of what he has revealed to others."[1]

Past Evangelical Interest in the Church Fathers

Thankfully, this has begun to change.[2] We who are evangelicals are beginning to grasp afresh that evangelicalism is, as Timothy George has rightly put it, "a renewal movement within historic Christian orthodoxy."[3] We have begun to rediscover that which many of our evangelical and Reformed forebears knew and treasured—the pearls of the ancient church. The French Reformer John Calvin (1509–1564), for example, was a keen student of the church fathers. He did not always agree with them, even his favorites, like Augustine of Hippo (354–430). But he was deeply aware of the value of knowing their thought and drawing upon the riches of their written works for elucidating the Christian faith in his own day.[4]

---

[1] *Commenting and Commentaries* (London: Passmore & Alabaster, 1876), 1. Cf. the similar remarks of J. I. Packer: "Tradition . . . is the fruit of the Spirit's teaching activity from the ages as God's people have sought understanding of Scripture. It is not infallible, but neither is it negligible, and we impoverish ourselves if we disregard it." "Upholding the Unity of Scripture Today," *Journal of the Evangelical Theological Society* 25 (1982): 414.

[2] Without necessarily agreeing with all that is said in the following, see, for example, James S. Cutsinger, ed., *Reclaiming the Great Tradition: Evangelicals, Catholics and Orthodox in Dialogue* (Downers Grove, IL: InterVarsity, 1997); D. H. Williams, *Retrieving the Tradition and Renewing Evangelicalism: A Primer for Suspicious Protestants* (Grand Rapids: Eerdmans, 1999); Stephen Holmes, *Listening to the Past: The Place of Tradition in Theology* (Grand Rapids: Eerdmans, 2002); D. H. Williams, *Evangelicals and Tradition: The Formative Influence of the Early Church* (Grand Rapids: Baker, 2005); Paul A. Hartog, ed., *The Contemporary Church and the Early Church: Case Studies in Resourcement* (Eugene, OR: Pickwick Papers, 2010).

[3] Endorsement in Williams, *Evangelicals and Tradition*, 1.

[4] See Anthony N. S. Lane, *John Calvin: Student of the Church Fathers* (Grand Rapids: Baker, 1999). For Calvin's view of Basil of Caesarea, for example, see D. F. Wright, "Basil the Great in the Protestant Reformers," in

In the following century, the Puritan theologian John Owen (1616–1683), rightly called by some the "Calvin of England,"[5] was not slow to turn to the experience of the one he called "holy Austin," namely Augustine, to provide him with a typology of conversion.[6] Yet again, the Particular Baptist John Gill (1697–1771) played a key role in preserving Trinitarianism among his fellow Baptists at a time when other Protestant bodies—for instance, the English Presbyterians, the General Baptists, and large tracts of Anglicanism—were unable to retain a firm grasp on this utterly vital biblical and Patristic doctrine. Gill's *The Doctrine of the Trinity Stated and Vindicated*[7] was an effective defense of the fact that there is "but one God; that there is a plurality in the Godhead; that there are three divine Persons in it; that the Father is God, the Son God, and the Holy Spirit God; that these are distinct in Personality, the same in substance, equal in power and glory."[8] But a casual perusal of this treatise reveals at once Gill's indebtedness to Patristic Trinitarian thought and exegesis, for he quotes such authors as Justin Martyr (d. ca. 165), Tertullian (fl. 190–220), and Theophilus of Antioch (fl. 170–180).

One final example of earlier evangelical appreciation of the Fathers must suffice. John Sutcliff (1752–1814), a late eighteenth-century English Baptist, was so impressed by the *Letter to Diognetus*, which he wrongly supposed to have been written by Justin Martyr, that he translated it for *The Biblical Magazine*, a Calvinistic publication with a small circulation. He sent it to the editor of this periodical with the commendation that this second-century work is "one of the most valuable pieces of ecclesiastical antiquity."[9]

Studia Patristica, ed. Elizabeth A. Livingstone (Oxford: Pergamon, 1982), 17/3:1149–50. For the Reformers' more general appreciation of the Fathers, see Geoffrey W. Bromiley, "The Promise of Patristic Studies," in David F. Wells and Clark H. Pinnock, eds., *Toward a Theology for the Future* (Carol Stream, IL: Creation House, 1971), 125–27. The same point was made by Ligon Duncan, "Did the Fathers Know the Gospel?," Together for the Gospel Conference, Louisville, Kentucky, April 15, 2010, accessed July 19, 2010, http://vimeo.com/10959890. Just as I am writing this, my attention has been drawn to a Roman Catholic response to Duncan's talk by Bryan Cross, "Ligon Duncan's 'Did the Fathers Know the Gospel?,'" *Called to Communion: Reformation Meets Rome* blog post, July 17, 2010. From the numerous responses to this post by Cross, it is evident that the study of the church fathers is an area of great interest today and a needed enterprise for evangelicals. I am thankful to Dr. Roger Duke for drawing my attention to this blog post.
[5] Allen C. Guelzo, "John Owen, Puritan Pacesetter," *Christianity Today*, May 21, 1976, 14.
[6] See *Pneumatologia: A Discourse Concerning the Holy Spirit*, vol. 3 of *The Works of John Owen*, ed. William H. Goold (repr., Edinburgh: Banner of Truth, 1965), 337–66.
[7] *The Doctrine of the Trinity Stated and Vindicated*, 2nd ed. (London: G. Keith and J. Robinson, 1752). The heart of this treatise was incorporated into Gill's *A Body of Doctrinal Divinity* (London, 1769), which became the major theological resource for many Baptist pastors on both sides of the Atlantic.
[8] Gill, *Doctrine of the Trinity*, 166–67.
[9] *The Biblical Magazine*, 2 (1802), 41–48. The quotation is from 41. On this letter, see below, chapter 3.

Who Are the Church Fathers?

In an entry on "patristics" in *The Oxford Dictionary of the Christian Church*, a standard reference work of Christianity, the church fathers are described as those authors who "wrote between the end of the 1st cent. . . . and the close of the 8th cent.," which comprises what is termed the "Patristic age." These authors, this entry continues,

> defended the Gospel against heresies and misunderstandings; they composed extensive commentaries on the Bible, explanatory, doctrinal, and practical, and published innumerable sermons, largely on the same subject; they exhibited the meaning and implications of the Creeds; they recorded past and current events in Church history; and they related the Christian faith to the best thought of their own age.[10]

In another major reference work dealing with Christianity's history and theology, *Christianity: The Complete Guide*, it is noted that while there is no official list of the Fathers, there are at least four characteristics that denote those meriting the title of church father: their orthodoxy of doctrine, their being accepted by the church as important links in the transmission of the Christian faith, their holiness of life, and their having lived between the end of the apostolic era (ca. 100) and the deaths of John of Damascus (ca. 655/675– ca. 749) in the East and Isidore of Seville (ca. 560–636) in the West.[11]

Recent study of the Fathers, this article goes on to observe, has tended to broaden the category of church father to include some figures many in the ancient church viewed with suspicion—namely, figures like Tertullian and Origen (ca. 185–254). This article also notes that, owing to the rise of feminist historiography, scholarship of this era is now prepared also to talk about church mothers ("matristics"). There is no doubt that feminist concerns have highlighted the way in which much of church history has been taught from an exclusively male perspective. But the problem with this category of "matristics" is that there are very few women in the ancient church who can be studied in similar depth to the Fathers since they left little textual remains.[12] In the chapters that follow, I briefly note the role played by Vibia Perpetua

---

[10] "Patristics," in F. L. Cross and E. A. Livingstone, eds., *The Oxford Dictionary of the Christian Church*, 3rd ed. (Oxford: Oxford University Press, 1997), 1233.

[11] "Church fathers," in John Bowden, ed., *Christianity: The Complete Guide* (Toronto: Novalis, 2005), 243–44.

[12] Ibid., 244. See, however, Patricia Cox Miller, *Women in Early Christianity: Translations from Greek Texts* (Washington, DC: The Catholic University of America Press, 2005).

(d. 202) and Macrina (ca. 327–ca. 379), for example; but, though I wish we had more detail about these fascinating women, any examination of them is bound by significant textual limitations.

Reading the Church Fathers for Freedom and Wisdom[13]

Why should evangelical Christians engage the thought and experience of these early Christian witnesses? First, study of the Fathers, like any historical study, liberates us from the present.[14] Every age has its own distinct outlook, presuppositions that remain unquestioned even by opponents. The examination of another period of thought forces us to confront our innate prejudices, which would go unnoticed otherwise. As contemporary historical theologian Carl Trueman has rightly noted:

> The very alien nature of the world in which the Fathers operated challenges us to think more critically about ourselves in our own context. We may not, for example, sympathise much with radically ascetic monasticism; but when we understand it as a fourth century answer to the age old question of what a committed Christian looks like at a time when it is starting to be easy and respectable, we can at least use it as an anvil on which to hammer out our own contemporary response to such a question.[15]

For instance, Gustaf Aulén, in his classic study of the atonement, *Christus Victor*, argues that an objective study of the Patristic concept of atonement will reveal a motif that has received little attention in post-Reformation Christianity: the idea of the atonement as a divine conflict and victory in which Christ fights and overcomes the evil powers of this world, under which man has been held in bondage. According to Aulén, what is commonly accepted as the New Testament doctrine of the atonement, the forensic theory of satisfaction, may in fact be a concept quite foreign to the New Testament. Whether his argument is right or not—and I think he is quite wrong—can be determined only by a fresh examination of the sources, both New Testament and Patristic.

---

[13] An earlier version of the next few paragraphs of this chapter has previously appeared as "Why Study the Fathers?," *Eusebeia: The Bulletin of The Andrew Fuller Center for Baptist Studies* 8 (Fall 2007): 3–7. Used by permission.

[14] C. S. Lewis, "De descriptione temporum," in Lewis, *Selected Literary Essays*, ed. Walter Hooper (Cambridge: Cambridge University Press, 1969), 12.

[15] "The Fathers," *Reformation 21* blog post, April 30, 2007, accessed July 23, 2010, http://www.reformation21.org/blog/2007/04/the-fathers.php.

Then, second, the Fathers can provide us with a map for the Christian life. It is indeed exhilarating to stand on the East Coast of North America, watch the Atlantic surf, hear the pound of the waves, and, if close enough, feel the salty spray. But this experience will be of little benefit in sailing to Ireland and the British Isles. For this a map is needed—a map based upon the accumulated experience of thousands of voyagers. Similarly, we need such a map for the Christian life. Experiences are fine and good, but they will not serve as a suitable foundation for our lives in Christ. To be sure, we have the divine Scriptures, an ultimately sufficient foundation for all of our needs as Christians (2 Tim. 3:16–17). But the thought of the Fathers can help us enormously in building on this foundation.

A fine example is provided by the pneumatology of Athanasius in his letters to Serapion, bishop of Thmuis. The present day has seen a resurgence of interest in the person of the Holy Spirit. This is admirable, but also fraught with danger if the Spirit is conceived of apart from Christ. Yet, Athanasius's key insight was that "from our knowledge of the Son we may be able to have true knowledge of the Spirit."[16] The Spirit cannot be divorced from the Son: not only does the Son send and give the Spirit, but also the Spirit is the principle of the Christ-life within us. Many have fallen into fanatical enthusiasm because they failed to realize this basic truth: the Spirit cannot be separated from the Son.

Or consider the landmark that has been set up on the landscape of church history by the Niceno-Constantinopolitan Creed, commonly called the Nicene Creed.[17] This document, while by no means infallible, is nevertheless a sure guide to the biblical doctrine of God. It should never be dismissed as being of no value. To do so shows a distinct lack of wisdom and discernment. I vividly recall a conversation in the 1990s with an administrator of an academic institution with which I was associated. During the conversation the subject of the Nicene Creed was raised, and this particular individual remarked cavalierly that there was no way he would be bound by a man-made document like this creed. Honestly, I was horrified by his dismissive approach and considered, and still do consider, such a statement to be the height of folly and the sure road to theological disaster.

---

[16]*Letter to Serapion* 3.5 (my translation).
[17]See below, chapter 6, for more details of this document.

Reading the Church Fathers so as to Understand the New Testament

Third, the Fathers may also, in some cases, help us to understand the New Testament. We have had too disparaging a view of Patristic exegesis and have come close to considering the exposition of the Fathers as a consistent failure to understand the New Testament.[18] For instance, Cyril of Jerusalem (ca. 315–387), in his interpretation of 1 Corinthians 7:5, which concerns temporary abstinence of sexual relations between married couples for the sake of prayer, assumes without question that the prayer is liturgical and communal.[19] Cyril may be guilty of an anachronism, for he was a leader in "the hallowing of the time," that is, the observance of holy seasons. Nonetheless, there is good evidence that such special communal times of prayer, in some form or other, are quite early. The liturgical life of the church of Jerusalem in the fourth century was not that of Corinth in the first, but nevertheless there were links. Possibly, it is the Protestant commentators who are guilty of anachronism when they assume that Paul meant private prayer. Such religious individualism is more conceivable in the Protestant West than in first-century Corinth.

Again, in recent discussions of the Pauline doctrine of salvation, it has been asserted by the proponents of the so-called New Perspective that the classical Reformed view of justification has little foundation in Paul or the rest of the New Testament, but is more a product of the thinking of Martin Luther (1483–1546) and John Calvin. Yet, in the second-century *Letter to Diognetus*, to which we have already referred, we find the following argument, which sounds like it has been lifted straight from the pages of Luther. The author has been arguing that God revealed his plan of salvation to none but his "beloved Son" until human beings realized their utter and complete inability to gain heaven by their own strength. Then, when men were conscious of their sin and impending judgment, God sent his Son, marked in his character by utter sinlessness, to die in the stead of humanity, who are indwelt by radical depravity.[20] What is expressed here is in full accord with the classical Reformed view of the meaning of Christ's death for our salvation. As T. F. Torrance has generally observed:

> [There is a] fundamental coherence between the faith of the New Testament and that of the early Church. . . . The failure to discern this coher-

---

[18]For a case study of Patristic exegesis, that of Origen, see chapter 4.

[19]*Catechesis* 4.25.

[20]For a more detailed discussion, see below, chapter 3.

ence in some quarters evidently has its roots in the strange gulf, imposed by analytical methods, between the faith of the primitive Church and the historical Jesus. In any case I have always found it difficult to believe that we modern scholars understand the Greek of the New Testament better than the early Greek Fathers themselves![21]

Reading the Church Fathers because of Bad Press about the Fathers

We also need to read and know the Fathers since they are sometimes subjected to simply bad history or bad press. For example, in Dan Brown's monumental best seller *The Da Vinci Code*, the hero, Robert Langdon, "discovers" that contemporary expressions of Christianity, especially that of the Roman Catholic Church, have no sound historical basis.[22] According to Brown's novel, it was not until the reign of the early fourth-century Roman emperor Constantine (ca. 272–337) that the Bible, in particular the New Testament, was collated. It was Constantine who had the New Testament as we know it drawn up in order to suppress an alternative perspective on Jesus as a merely human prophet.[23] The novel expresses the view that at the early fourth-century Council of Nicaea (325), which was astutely manipulated by the power-hungry Constantine for his own ends, Jesus Christ was "turned … into a deity" and became for the first time an object of worship. Jesus' divine status was ratified by a "relatively close vote" at this council.[24] Both of these events took place in order to conceal that Jesus was actually married to Mary Magdalene,[25] that he had a child by her,[26] and that he intended that Mary be the founder of the church.[27] Key Christian teachings are thus the result of a power move by Constantine and other males in order to squash women. As Brown has one of his characters say, "It was all about power."[28]

Brown clearly intends these claims to be more than key aspects of the conspiratorial ambience of his novel. As Greg Clarke, director of the Centre for Apologetic Scholarship and Education at New College, University of New South Wales, has rightly noted, Dan Brown's book has "evangelistic intentions"

[21]*Space, Time and Resurrection* (Grand Rapids: Eerdmans, 1976), xii.
[22]Gene Edward Veith, "The Da Vinci Phenomenon," *World*, May 20, 2006, 20–21. The edition of *The Da Vinci Code* cited here and below is *The Da Vinci Code* (New York: Anchor Books, 2006).
[23]*Da Vinci Code*, 231–32.
[24]Ibid., 233–35.
[25]Ibid., 244–47.
[26]Ibid., 255–56.
[27]Ibid., 248–49, 254.
[28]Ibid., 233.

and "is meant to change our lives."[29] R. Albert Mohler, president of the Southern Baptist Theological Seminary, rightly sees the book as a not-so-subtle attack on the central truths of biblical Christianity.[30] Since Brown makes clear references to the Patristic era to support his theory, it is necessary that any response involve accurate knowledge of what actually took place at Nicaea and what the second- and third-century church believed about Jesus.

Not only is Brown deeply mistaken about Nicaea, where the decision to embrace the Nicene Creed was overwhelmingly in favor of it, but the church in the second and third centuries had a very high christology in which Jesus Christ was worshipped as God.[31] One good example is the second-century preacher Melito of Sardis (d. ca. 190). Contemporaries regarded Melito as having lived a life remarkable for its spirituality, though knowledge of his career is scanty. Of his sixteen or so writings whose titles are known, only one is fully extant, the sermon *The Homily on the Passion*. Of the rest only fragments exist.[32] In his sermon, Melito, talking about Israel's failure to recognize who Christ was, says:

> You did not see God.
> You did not perceive the Lord, Israel,
> You did not recognize the first-born of God,
> Begotten before the morning star,
> Who adorned the light,
> Who lit up the day,
> Who divided the darkness,
> Who fixed the first boundary,
> Who hung the earth,
> Who tamed the abyss,
> Who stretched out the firmament,
> Who furnished the world,
> Who arranged the stars in the heavens,
> Who lit up the great lights,
> Who made the angels in heaven,

---

[29] *Is it Worth Believing? The Spiritual Challenge of The Da Vinci Code* (Kingsford, New South Wales: Matthias Media, 2005), 25.

[30] "Historical Propaganda," *Tabletalk*, May 2006, 12. This issue of *Tabletalk* is titled "The Da Vinci Hoax" and contains five articles devoted to examining Brown's book.

[31] See below, chapters 2 and 3, for the christology of Ignatius of Antioch and the *Letter to Diognetus*. This point was also made by Duncan, "Did the Fathers Know the Gospel?"

[32] On these writings, see *Melito of Sardis: On Pascha and Fragments*, trans. Stuart G. Hall (Oxford: Clarendon, 1979), 63–79.

Who there established thrones,
Who formed humanity on the earth.[33]

Here we see a rehearsal of Christ's sovereignty over creation, which, by implication, is a celebration of his deity. A little further on in the sermon Melito
explores the paradox of the cross and ends with an open confession of Christ's
deity:

He who hung the earth is hanging.
He who fixed the heavens in place has been fixed in place.
He who laid the foundations of the universe has been laid on a tree.
The Master has been profaned.
God has been murdered.[34]

As Bart Ehrman, himself no friend to orthodox Christianity, states in response
to Dan Brown, "Scholars who study the history of Christianity will find it
bizarre, at best, to hear [Brown] claim that Christians before the Council of
Nicaea did not consider Jesus to be divine."[35] Thus, when the creedal statement issued at Nicaea declared its belief in Jesus' divinity, it was simply affirming what had been the central conviction of the church between the apostolic
era and the time of the council itself.

Reading the Church Fathers as an Aid in Defending the Faith

The early centuries of the church saw Christianity threatened by a number of theological heresies: Gnosticism, Arianism, and Pelagianism, to name
but three. While history never repeats itself exactly, the essence of many of
these heresies has reappeared from time to time in the long history of Christianity. For instance, postmodernity's interest in spirituality, though it rages
against Christianity, has numerous similarities to the lengthy battle against
Gnosticism that occupied the church during the second and third centuries.
Knowledge of the way that Christians in the past defended the faith against

---

[33] *Homily on the Passion* 82, in *Melito of Sardis: On Pascha*, trans. Alistair Stewart-Sykes (Crestwood,
NY: St Vladimir's Seminary Press, 2001), 60.
[34] *Homily on the Passion* 96, in Stewart-Sykes, *Melito of Sardis*, 64. For a brief discussion of Melito's
christology, see pp. 28–29.
[35] Bart D. Ehrman, *Truth and Fiction in The Da Vinci Code: A Historian Reveals What We Really Know
about Jesus, Mary Magdalene, and Constantine* (Oxford: Oxford University Press, 2004), 15.

Gnosticism would provide helpful ways of responding to postmodern spirituality today.[36]

Or what about the challenge, one of the greatest of today, posed by Islam's attack on the Trinity and the deity of the Lord Jesus Christ?[37] Broadly speaking, evangelicals are woefully inadequate in their ability to respond to such an attack, for they rarely hear sermons on the Trinity and the incarnation. Here, the Fathers can help us enormously, for in replying to the Arians and then later to the Muslims they hammered out the biblical details of these two key doctrines. Consider the way that the theologian John of Damascus, also known as John Damascene or Yanah ibn Masur, a biblically informed Christian, responded to Islam during the early period of Muslim expansion.[38] In a small book defending the faith and worldview of Islam, Rana Kabbani identifies John as "the progenitor of a long tradition of Christian ridicule of Muhammad and the Qur'ān."[39] John does use some strong language about Islam, but it is clear that he has taken the time to understand Islamic views and thinking, and has even read the Qur'an in Arabic.[40]

As we noted above, John is often described as the last of the church fathers in the East, whose *The Fount of Knowledge* is the first great systematic theology to appear in the history of the church. He may very well have been an Arab by ethnicity, his family name being Masur, a name common among Syriac Christians of Arab descent.[41] His grandfather, Masur ibn Sargun, played a key role in the surrender of Damascus to the Muslim army of Khalid ibn al-Walid (d. ca. 641). Early rulers of Syria were tolerant of the presence of Christians, and John's grandfather became a key administrator in the Muslim government

---

[36] A good example in this regard is a DMin thesis by Rev. M. Todd Wilson of Munford, Tennessee, that I am currently supervising, "Back to the Future: Irenaeus as a Pastoral-Preaching Model for Answering Encroaching Neo-paganism in the Contemporary Evangelical Church" (DMin thesis, Knox Theological Seminary, forthcoming).

[37] For this point, I am indebted to a conversation with a close friend and my one-time student, Scott Dyer of Burlington, Ontario, July 2010.

[38] For the life and thought of John of Damascus, see the definitive study by Andrew Louth, *St. John Damascene: Tradition and Originality in Byzantine Theology* (Oxford: Oxford University Press, 2002). For brief sketches, see also Thomas FitzGerald, "John of Damascus," in *The Encyclopedia of Christianity*, ed. Erwin Fahlbusch et al., trans. Geoffrey W. Bromiley (Grand Rapids: Eerdmans; Leiden: E. J. Brill, 2003), 3:70–71; Bonifatius Kotter, "Johannes von Damaskus," in *Theologische Realenzyklopädie*, ed. Gerhard Müller (Berlin: Walter de Gruyter, 1988), 17:127–32. An English version of his writings is available in Frederic H. Chase Jr., *Saint John of Damascus: Writings*, The Fathers of the Church 37 (New York: Fathers of the Church, 1989).

[39] *Letter to Christendom* (London: Virago, 1989), 4.

[40] See Daniel J. Sahas, *John of Damascus on Islam: The "Heresy of the Ishmaelites"* (Leiden: E. J. Brill, 1972), passim; Louth, *St. John Damascene*, 76–83.

[41] Sahas, *John of Damascus on Islam*, 7.

of the region. John's father, Ibn Mansur, was known as an extremely devout Christian but also one of the most trusted officials in the Muslim regime. John succeeded his father as a key advisor to the Muslim ruler, Caliph Abd al-Malik (r. 685–705). After a long life of service in the public realm John left his public position in the early part of the eighth century in order to embrace a monastic lifestyle in a monastery near Jerusalem. John was a prolific writer, and among his writings there are two that address Islam: *On Heresies* 101, a lengthy section of a work that catalogs various heresies afflicting the church;[42] and *A Dialogue Between a Saracen and a Christian*.[43] Let us look briefly at the first of these works, *On Heresies* 101.

The text begins by defining Islam as the "still-prevailing superstition of the Ishmaelites that deceives people" and "the forerunner of the Antichrist." By describing Islam as "still-prevailing" John indicates the political dominance of Islam in his area of the world. However, he critiques it as a deceptive error and identifies it with the Antichrist, an identification that has long prevailed among Christian authors.

John then locates Muhammad historically and identifies some of his key theological teachings. Muhammad asserts, in John's words, that

> there is one God, the Maker of all things, neither having been begotten nor having begotten. He says Christ is the Word of God and His Spirit, only a creation and servant, and that he was born without seed from Mary the sister of Moses and Aaron. For he says the Word of God and the Spirit went into Mary and she bore Jesus who was a prophet and servant of God. And that the Jews, acting against the law, wanted to crucify him and having seized (him), they crucified his shadow. For Christ himself, they say, was not crucified nor did he die, for God took him to himself into heaven because he loved him.[44]

John here accurately relates the teaching of Islam that Christ was not crucified, but that "God raised him up to himself," which is actually an assertion inherited from Gnosticism![45] Obviously this assertion strikes at the heart of

---

[42] For translations, see Chase, *Saint John of Damascus*, 153–60; Sahas, *John of Damascus on Islam*, 133–41; and Kevin P. Edgecomb, "St. John of Damascus on Islam," *Biblicalia*, accessed September 7, 2007, http://www.bombaxo.com/blog/?p=210.

[43] For translations, see John W. Voorhis, "The Discussion of a Christian and a Saracen. By John of Damascus," *The Moslem World* 25 (1935): 266–73; Sahas, *John of Damascus on Islam*, 143–55.

[44] Edgecomb, "St. John of Damascus on Islam."

[45] Qur'an 4.157–58. Yet, there are two other texts, Qur'an 3.54–55 and 19.29–34, that imply that Christ died.

biblical Christianity, in which the death of Christ for sinners is absolutely central. If Christ did not die for our sins, human sin is unatoned for, there is no salvation, and obviously Christ has not been raised from the dead, nor will there be resurrection of all who believe in him. The Islamic teaching summarized by John also flies in the face of historical reality, for no serious historian doubts the reality of the crucifixion, whatever he might think of the Christian faith.[46]

John then goes on to deal with the Muslim critique of the Trinity.

> And they call us *Associaters*, because, they say, we introduce an associate to God by saying Christ is the Son of God and God. To whom we say that this is what the Prophets and Scripture have handed down. And you, as you insist, accept the Prophets. If, therefore, we are wrong saying Christ is the Son of God, they also are who taught and handed it down to us.[47]

Here John wrestles with the other key issue that Islam has with Christianity, namely its Trinitarianism. In some areas that had been Christian, Islam had an aesthetic appeal, namely, its utter simplicity as a monotheistic faith—God is one, and there is none other who is God—as opposed to Christianity with its complex theology with regard to the Trinity and the incarnation.[48] But as John rightly points out, Christian affirmation of the deity of Christ—and by extension the deity of the Holy Spirit—is found in the Scriptures. Christians are Trinitarian because the New Testament is Trinitarian. They therefore must seek to have some understanding of these truths, even though ultimately they escape human ability to fully comprehend.

John is clearly responding here to the declaration in the Qur'an that says:

---

[46]F. P. Cotterell, "The Christology of Islam," in *Christ the Lord*, ed. Harold H. Rowdon (Leicester: Inter-Varsity, 1982), 290–95, passim; Geoffrey Parrinder, *Jesus in the Qur'an* (New York: Barnes & Noble, 1965), 116.

[47]Edgecomb, "St. John of Damascus on Islam."

[48]The simplicity of Islam as opposed to Christianity's complexity is well seen in the architectural differences between churches from this era and mosques. The great church of S. Apollinaire that was built in the 530s near Ravenna in northern Italy, for example, is richly decorated with highly ornate mosaics designed to impress the observer and convince him or her that Christianity is a faith marked by "royal splendour." By contrast, the Great Mosque of Cordoba, built after the conquest of Visigothic Spain in the first two decades of the eighth century, is devoid of any images and extremely simple in design and ornamentation. This simplicity in architectural design matched the simplicity of Islamic theology and proved to be attractive to some. See Yoram Tsafrir, "Ancient Churches in the Holy Land," *Biblical Archaeology Review* 19, no. 5 (October 1993): 30; Robert Milburn, *Early Christian Art and Architecture* (Aldershot: Scholar Press, 1988), 173.

People of the Book, do not go to excess in your religion, and do not say anything about God except the truth: the Messiah, Jesus, son of Mary, was nothing more than a messenger of God, His word, conveyed to Mary, a spirit from Him. So believe in God and His messengers and do not speak of a "Trinity"—stop [this], that is better for you—God is only one God, He is far above having a son.[49]

We see here something of the fierce monotheism of Islam. John's response must ultimately be our response: But what does the New Testament claim and what does our Lord Jesus say of himself? Difficult to comprehend though the doctrine of the Trinity is, it is biblical truth and we need to know how to proclaim it.

In another text in which John of Damascus explicates the heart of the Christian faith, *The Orthodox Faith*, he says the following about the redemption that Christ has brought, and although he does not mention Islam explicitly, a clear contrast is being made between the two faiths: Since the coming of the Lord Jesus Christ,

altars and temples of idols have been overthrown. Knowledge of God has been implanted. The consubstantial Trinity, the uncreated Godhead is worshipped, one true God, Creator and Lord of all. Virtue is practiced. Hope of the resurrection has been granted through the resurrection of Christ. The demons tremble at the men who were formerly in their power. Yes, and most wonderful of all is that all these things were successfully brought about through a cross and suffering and death. The Gospel of the knowledge of God has been preached to the whole world and has put the adversaries to flight not by war and arms and camps. Rather, it was a few unarmed, poor, unlettered, persecuted, tormented, done-to-death men, who, by preaching One who had died crucified in the flesh, prevailed over the wise and powerful, because the almighty power of the Crucified was with them. That death which was once so terrible has been defeated and He who was once despised and hated is now preferred before life. These are the successes consequent upon the advent of the Christ; these are the signs of His power....

O Christ, O wisdom and power and Word of God, and God almighty! What should we resourceless people give You in return for all things? For all things are Yours and You ask nothing of us but that we be saved. [And]

---

[49]Qur'an 4.171. See also Qur'an 5.72–73 and 5.116–17, which include Mary in the Trinity.

even this You have given us, and by Your ineffable goodness You are gracious to those who accept it.[50]

Reading the Church Fathers for Spiritual Nurture

Christians, like all human beings, are historical beings. Their lives are inextricably tied to the past, their own immediate past and that of other humans. As Gilbert Beers, a past editor of *Christianity Today*, has noted, "We owe much to many whom we have never met." In times past, when there was a reverence for the past, this reality was acknowledged gratefully. But as Beers goes on to note, "We live in a throwaway society; we dispose of things we consider a burden. My concern is that we do not add our predecessors to the collection of throwaways, carelessly discarding those who have made us what we are."[51] The study of the church fathers, like the study of church history in general, informs Christians about their predecessors in the faith, those who have helped shape their Christian communities and thus make them what they are. Such study builds humility and modesty into the warp and woof of the Christian life and as such can exercise a deeply sanctifying influence.

In Hebrews 13:7, the author of this portion of Holy Scripture urges his readers to "remember" their past leaders, those who had spoken God's Word to them. They are to closely scrutinize (*anatheōrountes*) the "outcome"—"sum total" or "achievement" (*ekbasin*)—of their day-to-day behavior, manifested in a whole life.[52] Here is a key reason for studying the history of the church and the church fathers in particular. In the confessors and martyrs of the pre-Constantinian era, for example, we have many models of what it means to be a Christian in a hostile society, a situation that faces many believers around the world today, and increasingly so in the West.[53] And then during those days in the fourth century when the doctrine of the deity of Christ and his Spirit were under attack, we again have models of what it means to be committed to doctrinal fidelity. In this regard it is noteworthy that one of the fathers of Methodism, John Wesley (1703–1791), could cite the example of Athanasius's doggedness in defending the deity of Jesus in a letter of encouragement to the young abolitionist William Wilberforce (1759–1833). Writing but a week

---

[50] *An Exact Exposition of the Orthodox Faith* 4.4, in Chase, *Saint John of Damascus*, 338–39, altered.
[51] *Christianity Today*, November 26, 1982, 12.
[52] Philip Edgcumbe Hughes, *A Commentary on the Epistle to the Hebrews* (Grand Rapids: Eerdmans, 1977), 569; William L. Lane, *Hebrews 9–13*, Word Biblical Commentary 47b (Dallas: Word, 1991), 522.
[53] Trueman, "The Fathers."

before his death, the aged Christian evangelist told Wilberforce concerning his fight against the slave trade:

> Unless the Divine power has raised you up to be as an Athanasius *contra mundum*, I see not how you can go through your glorious enterprise, in opposing that execrable villainy which is the scandal of religion, of England, and of human nature. Unless God has raised you up for this very thing, you will be worn out by the opposition of men and devils; but if God be for you who can be against you. Are all of them together stronger than God? Oh be not weary of well-doing. Go on in the name of God, and in the power of His might, till even American slavery, the vilest that ever saw the sun, shall vanish away before it.[54]

Wesley begins this fascinating letter with a reference to Athanasius's defense of the deity of Christ for over thirty years despite exile and persecution. Athanasius was only able to maintain this fight, Wesley implies, because God enabled him to persevere. Likewise, unless God empowers Wilberforce in the struggle to abolish the institution of slavery, he will fall before those who support this "execrable villainy."

There is no doubt that generations of believers have found in the writings of men like Basil and Augustine soul-nourishing food, of which evangelicals in the past have been well aware. Wesley, for example, published a fifty-volume collection of spiritual classics, *The Christian Library* (1750), for his lay preachers. What is noteworthy is his inclusion of a number of Patristic spiritual classics: some of the writings of the apostolic fathers, the acts of early Christian martyrs, and the spiritually rich sermons of Macarius Symeon (fl. fourth century). Evangelical believers need to recapture the wisdom in this regard of our spiritual forebears.

This Book on the Church Fathers

These reasons are only a start toward giving a full answer to the question, why study the Fathers?[55] There are certainly other reasons for studying these ancient authors that may be more obvious or even more important. But the reasons given above sufficiently indicate the need for Patristic studies in the ongoing life of the church: to aid in her liberation from the Zeitgeist of the

---

[54]Frank Whaling, ed., *John and Charles Wesley: Selected Prayers, Hymns, Journal Notes, Sermons, Letters and Treatises* (New York: Paulist, 1981), 170–71.

[55]See further, Paul A. Hartog, "The Complexity and Variety of Contemporary Church–Early Church Engagements," in Hartog, *Contemporary Church and the Early Church*, 1–26.

twenty-first century; to provide a guide in her walk with Christ; to help her understand the basic witness to her faith, the New Testament; to refute bad histories of the ancient church; and to be a vehicle of spiritual nurture.

In this book, I seek to commend the reading and prayerful study of the church fathers by looking at several case studies, as it were. The specific church fathers that have been chosen—Ignatius of Antioch (fl. 80–107), the author of the *Letter to Diognetus*, Origen (ca. 185–254), Cyprian (ca. 200–258), Ambrose (ca. 339–397), Basil of Caesarea, and Patrick (ca. 389–ca. 461)—are men that I have listened to and walked with now for more than three decades.[56] But others could have served just as well as an introduction to the Fathers—men like Irenaeus of Lyons (ca. 130–ca. 200), Athanasius, or the other two Cappadocians besides Basil, Gregory of Nazianzus (ca. 329–389/390) and Gregory of Nyssa (ca. 335–ca. 394). What was critical was not primarily the choice of figures but the issues that they wrestled with in their lives as believers, for these issues are central to the Patristic era: martyrdom, monasticism, and discipleship; witness to an unbelieving world and mission; the canon and interpretation of Scripture; and the supreme issue of this era, the doctrine of the Trinity and worship.

One final word about the Fathers before we plunge into their world of long ago. The Fathers are not Scripture. They are senior conversation partners about Scripture and its meaning. We listen to them respectfully, but are not afraid to disagree when they err. As the Reformers rightly argued, the writings of the Fathers must be subject to Scripture. John Jewel (1522–1571), the Anglican apologist, put it well when he stated:

> But what say we of the fathers, Augustine, Ambrose, Jerome, Cyprian, etc.? What shall we think of them, or what account may we make of them? They be interpreters of the word of God. They were learned men, and learned fathers; the instruments of the mercy of God, and vessels full of grace. We despise them not, we read them, we reverence them, and give thanks unto God for them. They were witnesses unto the truth, they were worthy pillars and ornaments in the church of God. Yet may they not be compared with the word of God. We may not build upon them: we may not make them the foundation and warrant of our conscience: we may not put our trust in them. Our trust is in the name of the Lord.[57]

---

[56] See below, chapter 8, for reflection on this walk with the Fathers.
[57] Cited in Barrington R. White, "Why Bother with History?," *Baptist History and Heritage* 4 (July 1969): 85.

Chapter 2

DYING FOR CHRIST

The Thought of Ignatius of Antioch

What has happened to me has really served to advance the gospel,
so that it has become known throughout the whole imperial guard
and to all the rest that my imprisonment is for Christ.

PHILIPPIANS 1:12–13

In the seven letters of Ignatius of Antioch we possess one of the richest resources for understanding Christianity in the era immediately following that of the apostles.[1] Though somewhat staccato in style and filled with rhetorical embellishments, these letters manifest, in the words of biblical scholar Bruce Metzger, "such strong faith and overwhelming love of Christ as to make them one of the finest literary expressions of Christianity during the second century."[2]

A substantial portion of this chapter appeared as "'Come to the Father': Ignatius of Antioch and His Calling to Be a Martyr," *Themelios* 32, no. 3 (May 2007): 26–39. Used by permission. *Themelios* is now a digital journal operated by The Gospel Coalition. See http://www.thegospelcoalition.org/publications/?/themelios.

[1] Rowan Williams, *Christian Spirituality* (Atlanta: John Knox, 1980), 14.
[2] *The Canon of the New Testament: Its Origin, Development, and Significance* (Oxford: Clarendon, 1987), 44.

It is evident that three concerns were uppermost in Ignatius's mind as he wrote his letters.[3] First of all, he longed to see unity at every level in the life of the local churches to which he was writing. In his own words, he was a man "dedicated to the cause of unity."[4] It is important to note that this commitment to Christian unity did not override a passion for truth. Unity was unity in the gospel and in the Christian faith. Thus, his second major concern was an ardent desire that his fellow believers stand fast in their common faith against heresy. While there is no scholarly consensus as to the number of heresies in view in Ignatius's letters,[5] it is clear that one of them was a form of Docetism, which maintained that the incarnation of Christ, and consequently his death and resurrection, did not really take place. Finally, Ignatius was eager to recruit the help of his correspondents in the successful completion of his own vocation, which was nothing less than a call to martyrdom.[6]

All of these three areas of Ignatius's letters have occasioned both significant scholarly elaboration and sharp critique. Of the three, it is Ignatius's desire for martyrdom that has occasioned the most criticism as a number of scholars have suggested that Ignatius's remarks about his death reveal a man mentally unbalanced. W. H. C. Frend, in his monumental study *Martyrdom and Persecution in the Early Church*, describes Ignatius's letters as displaying "a state of exaltation bordering on mania,"[7] while G. E. M. de Ste. Croix bluntly states that Ignatius had "a pathological yearning" for

---

[3]John E. Lawyer Jr., "Eucharist and Martyrdom in the Letters of Ignatius of Antioch," *Anglican Theological Review* 73 (1991): 281. There have been debates about the authenticity of the letters. It was the Irish Calvinistic archbishop James Ussher (1581–1656) who pioneered the way to the modern perspective on what constitutes the authentic letters of Ignatius. See his *Polycarpi et Ignatii epistolae* (Oxford, 1644). On the transmission of the text of these letters, see also the brief summary by Andrew Louth, "Ignatius of Antioch," in *Early Christian Writings: The Apostolic Fathers*, trans. Maxwell Staniforth (1968; repr. Harmondsworth, UK: Penguin, 1987), 55–56; hereafter this translation will be cited as Staniforth, *Early Christian Writings*. On the authenticity, see also Christine Trevett, *A Study of Ignatius of Antioch in Syria and Asia* (Lewiston: Edwin Mellen, 1992), 9–15.

[4]Ignatius, *Philadelphians* 8.1, in Staniforth, *Early Christian Writings*, 95. See also Ignatius, *Polycarp* 1.2; *Philadelphians* 7.2.

[5]Thus, for example, Charles Thomas Brown, *The Gospel and Ignatius of Antioch* (New York: Peter Lang, 2000), 176–97, believes that there are two heretical groups in view, Gentile Judaizers and Gnostics. If so, the first group is addressed in *Magnesians* and *Philadelphians*, while the Gnostics are responded to in *Trallians* and *Smyrnaeans*. For other helpful contributions to this discussion, see L. W. Barnard, "The Background of St. Ignatius of Antioch," *Vigiliae Christianae* 17 (1963): 193–206; Trevett, *Study of Ignatius of Antioch*, 194–99; Jerry L. Sumney, "'Those Who 'Ignorantly Deny Him': The Opponents of Ignatius of Antioch," *Journal of Early Christian Studies* 1 (1993): 345–65.

[6]It is noteworthy that Ignatius never uses the term *martyrs* as a technical term.

[7]*Martyrdom and Persecution in the Early Church* (Oxford: Basil Blackwell, 1965), 197.

death, the sure sign of "an abnormal mentality."[8] A careful study, though, of Ignatius's thinking about his own death reveals a man who rightly knew that Christian believing demands passionate engagement of the entire person, even to the point of physical death. To borrow some words from contemporary theologian Kevin Vanhoozer, martyrdom for Ignatius was "a powerful form of truth-disclosive action," namely, the truth about Christ and about himself as a Christian.[9]

In a study of the differences between Ignatius's letters, Mikael Isacson has rightly noted that Ignatius's letters to the Romans and to Polycarp (69/70–155/156) are substantially different from the other five. The letter to Polycarp is the only one addressed to an individual and contains mostly a series of pastoral exhortations from one bishop to another. The letter to the Romans is to a church with which Ignatius has no personal link, unlike the other five churches to which he sends letters. With regard to its content, it is extremely focused: it is on his impending martyrdom.[10] Ignatius's martyr-centered letter to the Romans thus will be the focus of the central section of this chapter.[11]

It is also noteworthy that the letter to the Romans has no salutation to a bishop at Rome. In all of the other letters, Ignatius speaks of the bishop of the congregation to which he is writing, but not in his letter to Rome. Whatever the reason for this omission, what is clear is that in Ignatius's ecclesiology, the bishop is vital to the unity of the local church.[12] Thus, for example, the only valid celebration of the Lord's Supper is the one over which the bishop presides.[13] And only the marriage that takes place with the consent of the bishop can be described as a Christian marriage (*kata kyrion*).[14] In reading such statements about the episcopacy, it is important to remember the context in which they are being made. The communities to which Ignatius is writing are wrestling with the presence of heresy, and Ignatius is convinced that one

---

[8]"Why Were the Early Christians Persecuted?," *Past and Present* 26 (November 1963): 23–24. He further suggests that Ignatius is the precursor of a type of early Christian martyr heavily critiqued by church leaders, namely, the voluntary martyr (ibid.). There is no evidence to support this suggestion.

[9]*First Theology: God, Scripture and Hermeneutics* (Downers Grove, IL: InterVarsity; Leicester, England: Apollos, 2002), 364–65.

[10]*To Each Their Own Letter: Structure, Themes, and Rhetorical Strategies in the Letters of Ignatius of Antioch* (Stockholm: Almqvist & Wiksell, 2004), 20.

[11]For the phrase *martyr-centered*, I am indebted to Lucy Grig, *Making Martyrs in Late Antiquity* (London: Duckworth, 2004), 16.

[12]See, for example, *Magnesians* 13.1–2; *Smyrnaeans* 8–9; *Philadelphians* 7.1–2; *Polycarp* 6.1.

[13]*Smyrnaeans* 8.1.

[14]*Polycarp* 5.2.

orthodox leader in the congregation, the bishop, can secure that congregation's orthodoxy. It is not the case, at least to this reader of Ignatius's letters, that the bishop of Antioch is "overly enchanted with the idea of monepiscopacy *per se*."[15]

Given Ignatius's concern to rebut heresy, it is not surprising to find him linking the themes of martyrdom and christological orthodoxy. This link is primarily made in the letter to the Smyrnaeans and will be examined near the close of this chapter. First, though, how persecution of Christians like Ignatius arose needs to be outlined, and then, second, what can be known about Ignatius's journey to Rome and the immediate historical context of his letters needs to be laid out.

The Christian Martyr

Our word *martyr* is derived from the Greek *martys*, originally a juridical term that was used of a witness in a court of law. Such a person "has direct knowledge or experience of certain persons, events or circumstances and is therefore in a position to speak out and does so."[16] In the New Testament the term and its cognates are frequently applied to Christians, who bear witness to Christ, often in real courts of law, when his claims are disputed and their fidelity is tested by persecution.

The transition of this word within the early Christian communities from "witness" to what the English term *martyr* entails is an excellent gauge of what was happening to Christians as they bore witness to Christ in the first century. In Acts 1:8 Jesus tells the apostles that they will be his "witnesses" (*martyres*) in Jerusalem, Judea, Samaria, and to the ends of the earth. At this point the word does not have the association of death, although in Acts 22:20 we do read of the "blood of Stephen," the Lord's "witness," being shed. But it is really not until the end of the writing of the New Testament canon that the term *martys* has acquired the association with death.[17]

At the end of the apostolic era, the risen Christ in Revelation 2 commends his servant Antipas, his "faithful witness," who was slain for the Christian faith at Pergamum, "where Satan dwells" (Rev. 2:12–13). Pergamum, it should be

---

[15]Kenneth A. Strand, "The Rise of the Monarchical Episcopate," *Andrews University Seminary Studies* 4 (1966): 77. For an illuminating discussion of Ignatius's view of the leadership of the local church, see Allen Brent, "The Ignatian Epistles and the Threefold Ecclesiastical Order," *The Journal of Religious History* 17, no. 1 (June 1992): 18–32.

[16]Allison A. Trites, *The New Testament Concept of Witness* (Cambridge: Cambridge University Press, 1977), 9.

[17]Cf. G. W. Bowersock, *Martyrdom and Rome* (Cambridge: Cambridge University Press, 1995), 1–21.

noted, was a key center of emperor worship in Asia Minor, the first town in the province to build a temple to a Roman emperor, namely Augustus Caesar. It may well have been Antipas's refusal to confess Caesar as Lord and worship him that led to his martyrdom.[18] The word *martys* seems thus to have acquired its future meaning first in the Christian communities in Asia Minor, where the violent encounter between church and empire was particularly intense.[19] In this regard, it is certainly not fortuitous that Asia Minor was "unusually fond" of the violent entertainment of the gladiatorial shows. There was, in fact, a training school for gladiators at Pergamum. Along with this fascination with such violence there would have been a demand for victims over and above the requisite gladiators. Thus, recourse was had to killing Christians, among others.[20] And so the word *martys* became restricted in its usage to a single signification: bearing witness to the person and work of Christ to the point of death.

Jewish and Roman Persecution of the Church

Initially, violence against the church came not from the Roman state but from Jesus' own people, the Jews. This fact is well illustrated by the incident recorded in Acts 18:12–16, when some of the Jewish leaders seek to enlist the help of the Roman state to expel the apostle Paul from Corinth. They bring their case to the proconsul of Achaia, Lucius Junius Gallio (d. 65), the older brother of Seneca (d. 65), the mentor and advisor of the emperor Nero (37–68), and accuse the apostle of teaching people to worship God in ways that violate Roman law. But contrary to their expectation, as the narrative relates, Gallio clearly regards the quarrel between the Jews and the apostle Paul as something internal to Judaism and of no real concern to the Roman government. In this passage the attack on the church comes from those Jews who refuse to accept the message that the crucified and risen Jesus is the longed-for Messiah.

---

[18]Paul Keresztes, "The Imperial Roman Government and the Christian Church. I. From Nero to the Severi," in *Aufstieg und Niedergang der römischen Welt*, 2.23.1, ed. Wolfgang Haase (Berlin: Walter de Gruyter, 1979), 272; G. K. Beale, *The Book of Revelation* (Grand Rapids: Eerdmans, 1999), 246. In contrast to what I have argued about this being a case of the later technical usage of *martys*, Bowersock (*Martyrdom and Rome*, 14–15) maintains that Antipas was not a *martys* "because he was slain, but a witness who was slain."

[19]Thus Theofried Baumeister, "Martyrdom and Persecution in Early Christianity," trans. Robert Nowell, in *Martyrdom Today*, ed. Johannes-Baptist Metz and Edward Schillebeeckx (Edinburgh: T&T Clark; New York: Seabury, 1983), 4.

[20]Bowersock, *Martyrdom and Rome*, 17–18; Keresztes, "Imperial Roman Government and the Christian Church," 272.

In fact, throughout the early days of Christianity, as they are recorded in the book of Acts, it is the Jews who attack the church. It is they who jail the apostles Peter and John and threaten them with punishment if they preach in the name of Jesus (Acts 4:1–22). A short time later, they jail all of the apostles, flog them, and then order them again not to preach in Jesus' name (Acts 5:17–41). It is they who kill Stephen, the first martyr (Acts 7). One of the chief Jewish persecutors is Saul/Paul, who, on his way to Damascus to harass the church with the hope of destroying it, is stopped midstream and turned into a lover of the Jesus, whom he had hated (Acts 9:1–19). When this former persecutor now turned Christian preacher begins to proclaim Jesus as the Messiah, the Jewish leaders, both in Damascus and in Jerusalem, seek to kill him (Acts 9:22–25, 29). It is the half-Jewish Herod Agrippa who slays the apostle James and imprisons Peter with every intention of doing the same to him (Acts 12:1–19). Then, as Luke follows the ministry of Paul in Gentile cities and towns, it is Jewish synagogue leaders who again and again prove to be the fiercest opponents of the gospel.[21]

By the mid-60s, however, during the reign of the Roman emperor Nero, the picture was totally different. In mid-July of 64, a fire began in the heart of the city of Rome that raged out of control for nearly a week and gutted most of the city. After it had been extinguished, it was rumored that Nero himself had started it, for it was common knowledge that Nero wanted to level the capital of the empire in order to rebuild the city in a style in keeping with his conception of his own greatness. Conscious that he had to allay suspicions that he was responsible for the fire, Nero fixed the blame on the Christians.[22] A number of Christians, including the apostle Peter according to early Christian tradition, a tradition that seems to be genuine,[23] were arrested and executed. Their crime was ostensibly arson. Roman historian Tacitus (ca. 56–ca. 120) seems to doubt the reality of this, though he does believe that Christians are rightly "loathed for their vices." Tacitus's text mentions

---

[21]See, for example, Acts 13:44–50; 14:1–6, 19–20; 17:1–9, 13–14; 18:12–16; 19:8–9; 20:19; 21:10–14, 27–36; 22:22–23; 23:12–22.

[22]The fullest description that we have of this violence against the church is from the Roman historian, Tacitus. See his *Annals* 15.44.3–8. For a discussion of this important account by Tacitus, see Paul Winter, "Tacitus and Pliny on Christianity," *Klio* 52 (1970): 497–502; Keresztes, "Imperial Roman Government and the Christian Church," 247–57; Stephen Benko, "Pagan Criticism of Christianity During the First Two Centuries A.D.," in *Aufstieg und Niedergang der römischen Welt*, 2.23.2, ed. Wolfgang Haase (Berlin: Walter de Gruyter, 1980), 1062–68; Ivor J. Davidson, *The Birth of the Church: From Jesus to Constantine, A.D. 30–312*, The Baker History of the Church 1 (Grand Rapids: Baker, 2004), 191–93.

[23]See Tertullian, *Scorpiace (Antidote to the Scorpion's Sting)* 15.

only one vice explicitly: "hatred of the human race." Why would Christians, who preached a message of divine love and who were commanded to love even their enemies, be accused of such a vice? Well, if one looks at it through the eyes of Roman paganism, the logic seems irrefutable. It was, after all, the Roman gods who kept the empire secure. But the Christians refused to worship these gods—thus the charge of "atheism" that was sometimes leveled at them.[24] Therefore, many of their pagan neighbors reasoned, they could not love the emperor or the empire's inhabitants. Christians thus were viewed as fundamentally anti-Roman and so a positive danger to the empire.[25] And one of the most prominent Christians killed in the early second century by the Roman imperium as an enemy of the state was Ignatius, bishop of the church in Antioch of Syria.

Ignatius's Physical Journey to Rome

Ignatius was arrested in the city of Antioch somewhere between 107 and 110 and sent to Rome for trial.[26] There are no details of the persecution in which he was arrested, though Ignatius does mention others who were probably arrested during the same persecution and who had preceded him to Rome.[27] He was taken across the great roads of southern Asia Minor in the custody of ten Roman soldiers, whom he likened to "savage leopards."[28] He expected the end of the journey in Rome to have one certain outcome: death.

Yet, there is a difficulty concerning certain details of his arrest. Since Ignatius was on his way to Rome for execution, this would suggest that he was a Roman citizen because a citizen's right to trial by the emperor was, at this

---

[24]See, for example, Justin Martyr, 2 Apology 3; Athenagoras, Plea on Behalf of the Christians 3.1; 10.5; 13.1.

[25]Christians were also charged with incest, seemingly a misunderstanding of the common Christian statement about loving their brothers and sisters in Christ, and cannibalism, a misunderstanding of the Lord's Table. See, in regard to the latter, for instance, Justin Martyr, 2 Apology 12. Pliny, Letters 10.96, also views Christians as being guilty of "fanaticism" (amentia) and wanton and prolonged disobedience (contumacia) to Roman magistrates who commanded them to worship the Roman gods. See the similar charge by Marcus Aurelius, Meditations 11.3. For an excellent study of the pagan accusations against Christianity, see especially Jakob Engberg, Impulsore Chresto: Opposition to Christianity in the Roman Empire c. 50–250 AD, trans. Gregory Carter, Early Christianity in the Context of Antiquity 2 (Frankfurt am Main: Peter Lang GmbH, 2007).

[26]For the date, see Trevett, Study of Ignatius of Antioch, 3–9.

[27]Ignatius, Romans 10.2. Polycarp, in his sole surviving letter, mentions the names of two of these prisoners, Zosimus and Rufus. Philippians 9.1.

[28]Ignatius, Romans 5.1. This is the earliest occurrence of the word for leopard in Greek. See D. B. Saddington, "St Ignatius, Leopards, and the Roman Army," Journal of Theological Studies 38 (1987): 411.

stage in Roman history, a firmly established right.[29] However, some modern scholars have asked why, if he was a citizen, he said that he was expecting to meet "fire, cross, beast-fighting"[30] when he reached Rome, since it has been believed that these forms of punishment were not used in the execution of citizens at this time.[31] In general, Roman punishment was measured to fit the social status of the criminal rather than the nature of the crime. In the words of Ramsey MacMullen, "Everything depended on status."[32] Thus, beheading or the opportunity to commit suicide were the major forms of execution for those upper-class citizens of the empire who had committed a capital offense. But others, noncitizens of the lower classes, would be exposed to a whole range of horrific violence, including burning, being forced to drink molten lead, being crucified, being beaten to death, and being mauled to death by dogs and ferocious beasts.[33] Yet, as Peter Garnsey and MacMullen have pointed out, citizens of the lower classes could also be exposed to these latter forms of punishments, especially as the second century wore on.[34] This might imply that while Ignatius was a citizen, he may well have come from the lower classes.

The road Ignatius probably traveled, the main highway across southern Asia Minor, ran westward to Ephesus, where travelers, or in this case a prisoner, would take a ship to go either directly to Italy or on up the coast to Troas. Near Laodicea, though, his guards turned north and west to Philadelphia and later to Smyrna, where Ignatius apparently stayed for some time. Polycarp, recently appointed bishop of Smyrna, sought to minister to his needs upon his arrival in that town. When he came to Smyrna there were also representatives of three other churches to meet him. Damas, the bishop of the church in Magnesia-on-the-Meander, had come along with

[29]F. F. Bruce, *The Book of Acts*, rev. ed. (Grand Rapids: Eerdmans, 1988), 453–54, 454n11. Compare Pliny, *Letters* 10.96.3–4, who also mentions sending imprisoned Christians to Rome for trial.

[30]Ignatius, *Romans* 5.3, in Staniforth, *Early Christian Writings*, 87.

[31]Trevett, *Study of Ignatius of Antioch*, 5.

[32]Ramsey MacMullen, "Judicial Savagery in the Roman Empire," *Chiron* 16 (1986): 147.

[33]For the range of punishments, see ibid., 147–66. For the punishments to which Christians were subject, see Elaine H. Pagels, "Gnostic and Orthodox Views of Christ's Passion: Paradigms for the Christian's Response to Persecution?" in *The Rediscovery of Gnosticism*, vol. 1, *The School of Valentinus*, ed. Bentley Layton (Leiden: E. J. Brill, 1980), 266–70.

[34]Peter Garnsey, "Legal Privilege in the Roman Empire," *Past and Present* 41 (December 1968): 3–24; MacMullen, "Judicial Savagery in the Roman Empire," 149–53. See also the larger study by Peter Garnsey, *Social Status and Legal Privilege in the Roman Empire* (Oxford: Clarendon, 1970); and Elizabeth A. Castelli, *Martyrdom and Memory: Early Christian Culture Making* (New York: Columbia University Press, 2004), 39–41.

two elders from his church, Bassus and Apollonius, and a deacon, Zotion.[35] From Tralles came the bishop Polybius,[36] and from Ephesus a number of leaders: Onesimus the bishop, a deacon by the name of Burrhus, and Crocus, Euplus, and Fronto.[37]

It was at Smyrna that Ignatius wrote the letter to the Roman Church,[38] which contains the heart of his reflection about his martyrdom. This is the only letter of Ignatius's that is dated. He was writing it, he tells the Roman believers, on the ninth day before the kalends of September, that is, August 24.[39] Obviously a date is included because he wishes to give the church at Rome some idea of when to expect him.[40] Not long after writing this letter to the Roman Church the Antiochene bishop left Smyrna for Troas. This stage in Ignatius's journey is not clear: the soldiers took him to Troas either by road or by a vessel that would have sailed within sight of the shore. We are also uncertain as to how long they stopped at Troas.[41] Ignatius, however, was able to write three more letters from there: letters to the churches at Philadelphia and Smyrna, and finally one to the man who befriended him in Smyrna, Polycarp.[42]

The Roman soldiers and their Christian prisoner seem to have left Troas in something of a hurry and made their way to Neapolis in Macedonia.[43] From there they would have passed through Philippi to Dyrrachium, on what is now the Adriatic coast.[44] From Dyrrachium they probably would have taken another ship for Brundisium in Italy and then by land made their way to Rome. At this point a curtain is drawn across the historical events, and nothing more of Ignatius's earthly career is known for certain, except the report by Polycarp to the church at Philippi that he was martyred, presumably at Rome.[45]

---

[35] Ignatius, *Magnesians* 2.

[36] Ignatius, *Trallians* 1.1.

[37] Ignatius, *Ephesians* 1.3–2.1. It has been argued that the Onesimus here is none other than the slave Onesimus referred to in Paul's letter to Philemon. The name, however, is a common one, and it is unlikely that it is the same person. See William R. Schoedel, *Ignatius of Antioch: A Commentary on the Letters of Ignatius of Antioch*, ed. Helmut Koester (Philadelphia: Fortress, 1985), 43–44.

[38] Ignatius, *Romans* 10.1.

[39] Ignatius, *Romans* 10.3.

[40] Virginia Corwin, *St. Ignatius and Christianity in Antioch* (New Haven, CT: Yale University Press, 1960), 14–17.

[41] Ibid., 17.

[42] Ignatius, *Philadelphians* 11.2; *Smyrnaeans* 12.1; *Polycarp* 8.1.

[43] Ignatius, *Polycarp* 8.1.

[44] For the mention of Ignatius passing through Philippi, see Polycarp, *Philippians* 1.1.

[45] Corwin, *St. Ignatius and Christianity in Antioch*, 18. See Polycarp, *Philippians* 9.1 for the report of Ignatius's death.

The Spiritual Journey

As Ignatius's remarks about martyrdom in his letters are read, one fact above all must be kept in mind. In the words of William C. Weinrich, "Ignatius [here] reflects upon *his own* coming martyrdom."[46] This explains the passionate nature of some of his statements. It also means that we should not take these letters to be a systematic theology on martyrdom.[47] Ignatius speaks for himself and about himself. Again, Weinrich comments, "What he says, he says about himself as one who is going into death because he is a Christian."[48]

It would appear that Ignatius is aware that certain individuals in the Roman Christian community, who came from fairly high social circles in Rome, have "connections" and political influence that they can exercise so as to get Ignatius released.[49] If Ignatius says nothing to these believers to dissuade them from using their influence, he fears that they may well try to have him freed and may even succeed in this endeavor. Since he does not want this (for reasons detailed below), he decides to speak. "What fills me with fear," he tells these politically influential believers at Rome, "is your own kindly feeling for me." It might be easy for them to intervene to have Ignatius released, but this will only make it more difficult for him "to get to God." He thus urges the Roman Christians, "Keep your lips sealed." If they do, then they will enable Ignatius to become "a word of God."[50] In other words, the silence of the Roman believers will mean that Ignatius, by his martyrdom, can proclaim to the world the sincerity of his faith. Ignatius's claim to be a Christian will then be seen to be more than mere words. It will be authenticated by deeds—in this case, the act of martyrdom.[51] The authenticity of Ignatius's faith will be revealed by his dying well.

In spelling out how he wants the Roman believers to act, Ignatius reveals the conviction that he views his martyrdom not as an individual event, but as one that involves the entire Roman Church.[52] The Roman believers are

---

[46]William C. Weinrich, *Spirit and Martyrdom: A Study of the Work of the Holy Spirit in Contexts of Persecution and Martyrdom in the New Testament and Early Christian Literature* (Washington, DC: University Press of America, 1981), 115. This is an excellent study of early Christian thinking about the pneumatology of martyrdom, and I am deeply indebted to a number of Weinrich's insights.

[47]Pace Williams, *Christian Spirituality*, 14.

[48]Weinrich, *Spirit and Martyrdom*, 115–16.

[49]Corwin, *St. Ignatius and Christianity in Antioch*, 23–24; Peter Lampe, *From Paul to Valentinus: Christians at Rome in the First Two Centuries*, trans. Michael Steinhauser, ed. Marshall D. Johnson (Minneapolis: Fortress, 2003), 88–89.

[50]Ignatius, *Romans* 1.2–2.1, in Staniforth, *Early Christian Writings*, 85.

[51]Ignatius, *Romans* 2. See also Schoedel, *Ignatius of Antioch*, 171.

[52]Weinrich, *Spirit and Martyrdom*, 134–35.

not mere bystanders who are simply expected to allow something to happen. Both Ignatius and the believers at Rome must choose either to act out the implications of Christ's passion or to desire the world. Thus, he tells them:

> It is the hope of this world's prince to get hold of me and undermine my resolve, set as it is upon God. Pray let none of you lend him any assistance, but take my part instead, for it is the part of God. Do not have Jesus Christ on your lips, and the world in your heart; do not cherish thoughts of grudging me my fate. Even if I were to come and implore you in person, do not yield to my pleading; keep your compliance for this written entreaty instead.[53]

For the Roman believers to enable Ignatius to attain to his calling of martyrdom is, in a very real sense, to share in that suffering with him.[54]

But there is another request here. Ignatius knows that he is no superman. He is a man with a vivid imagination who can well envision the sort of death that awaits him at Rome. As he says earlier in the letter:

> Leave me to be a meal for the beasts, for it is they who can provide my way to God. I am his wheat, ground fine by the lions' teeth to be made purest bread. . . . Fire, cross, beast-fighting, hacking and quartering, splintering of bone and mangling of limb, even the pulverizing of my entire body—let every horrid and diabolical torment come upon me, provided only that I can win my way to Jesus Christ![55]

Ignatius is afraid that at the last his courage may fail and that he will ask the Roman believers to get him freed. Thus, he tells them, do not listen to me if that happens: "Even if I were to come and implore you in person, do not yield to my pleading; keep your compliance for this written entreaty instead."[56] Given his fears, it is quite understandable that he asks the Romans to pray for him. "The only petition I would have you put forward on my behalf," he asks them, "is that I may be given sufficient inward and outward strength to be as resolute in will as in words." Again, near the end of the letter he pleads with them, "Intercede for me that I may have my wish."[57] Ignatius's request

---

[53]Ignatius, *Romans* 7.1–2, in Staniforth, *Early Christian Writings*, 87.
[54]Ignatius, *Romans* 6; Weinrich, *Spirit and Martyrdom*, 135–36.
[55]Ignatius, *Romans* 4.1; 5.3, in Staniforth, *Early Christian Writings*, 86, 87.
[56]Ignatius, *Romans* 7.2, in Staniforth, *Early Christian Writings*, 87.
[57]Ignatius, *Romans* 3.2; 8.3, in Staniforth, *Early Christian Writings*, 86, 88.

for prayer for perseverance bespeaks the realization that true faith is found to be genuine only in the place of endurance.[58]

Martyrdom as Imitation and Renunciation

Why, though, is he willing to die? First, Ignatius is certain that his martyrdom will please God. As he declares with confidence about his desire to die for Christ: "I am not writing now as a mere man, but I am voicing the mind of God."[59] The use of genitives in his description of himself as "his [i.e., God's] wheat" and "the purest bread for Christ"[60] reveals Ignatius's awareness that "God is the author of martyrdom." Consequently he must be pleased with those who die for the sake of their faith in Christ.[61]

Why exactly does Ignatius's martyrdom please God? First of all, he conceives of it as an imitation of the death of Christ. "Leave me to imitate the passion of my God," he says at one point.[62] If God the Father was pleased with his Son's death for sinners, Ignatius's dying for his faith in Christ is also pleasing to God. Just as Christ's death was one in which violence was done to him, but he did not retaliate,[63] likewise is the death of Ignatius, the imitator of his Lord's passion. Weinrich rightly notes, though, that there is not the slightest hint that Ignatius's death has any salvific value for others as Christ's death has.[64]

Noteworthy in the text just cited is Ignatius's high christology. In referring to Christ as "God," Ignatius evidently expects the Christians in Rome to be both familiar with a high christology and comfortable with it.[65] This text also bears witness to a common way early Christian theologians talked about Christ: Ignatius attributes to one and the same person, Jesus Christ, divine and human characteristics. For example, Jesus is declared to be God, but he is also said to suffer. This exchange of divine and human attributes is

---

[58]See Vanhoozer, *First Theology*, 368.

[59]Ignatius, *Romans* 8.3, in Staniforth, *Early Christian Writings*, 88. See also *Romans* 2.1, where he is urging the Roman Church to allow his martyrdom to take place: "It is not men I want you to gratify, but God." In Staniforth, *Early Christian Writings*, 85.

[60]Ignatius, *Romans* 4.1, in Staniforth, *Early Christian Writings*, 86.

[61]Weinrich, *Spirit and Martyrdom*, 115.

[62]Ignatius, *Romans* 6.3, in Staniforth, *Early Christian Writings*, 87.

[63]See, for example, 1 Pet. 2:21–23.

[64]Weinrich, *Spirit and Martyrdom*, 112–13. Thus Weinrich comments, "It is . . . quite doubtful whether Ignatius conceived of his martyrdom as sacrificially vicarious for his fellow Christians" (113). Compare this with Frend, *Martyrdom and Persecution in the Early Church*, 199.

[65]See also the following texts where Ignatius describes Christ as God: *Romans*, Salutation, 6.3; *Ephesians*, Salutation, 1.1, where Ignatius refers to the "blood of God"; 18.2; *Smyrnaeans* 1.1.

possible only because they are being predicated of a single subject.[66] Thus, Ignatius can say of Christ:

> There is only one Physician—
> Very flesh, yet Spirit too;
> Uncreated, and yet born;
> God-and-Man in One agreed,
> Very-Life-in-Death indeed,
> Fruit of God and Mary's seed;
> At once impassible and torn
> By pain and suffering here below:
> Jesus Christ, whom as our Lord we know.[67]

Martyrdom is also the expression of and culmination to Ignatius's ultimate renunciation of the world. As he states, "All the ends of the earth, all the kingdoms of the world would be of no profit to me; so far as I am concerned, to die in Jesus Christ is better than to be monarch of earth's widest bounds."[68] Martyrdom vividly brought to the fore a key theme of much of early Christian teaching and conviction: the world, in this case the world of the Roman Empire, was a friend neither of the church nor of her God.[69] However, it is curious, as Frend points out, that apart from the reference to the soldiers guarding him as "savage leopards," Ignatius says nothing directly about the empire.[70]

One of Ignatius's most powerful evocations of this theme of renunciation comes in the following declaration in his letter to Rome: "Earthly longings [*ho emos erōs*] have been crucified and in me there is left no spark of desire for mundane things, but only a murmur of living water that whispers within me, 'Come to the Father.'"[71] The reference here to the "living water" is

---

[66]Aloys Grillmeier, *Christ in Christian Tradition*, vol. 1, *From the Apostolic Age to Chalcedon (451)*, trans. John Bowden, 2nd ed. (Atlanta: John Knox, 1975), 89; Thomas Weinandy, "Ignatius of Antioch," in *The New Lion Handbook: The History of Christianity* (Oxford: Lion Hudson, 2007), 51.

[67]Ignatius, *Ephesians* 7.2, in Staniforth, *Early Christian Writings*, 63.

[68]Ignatius, *Romans* 6.1, in Staniforth, *Early Christian Writings*, 87. Frend sees in this statement an echo of Paul's statement in Phil. 1:21, "For to me to live is Christ, and to die is gain" (*Martyrdom and Persecution in the Early Church*, 198). On this theme of martyrdom and renunciation, see David A. Lopez, *Separatist Christianity: Spirit and Matter in the Early Church Fathers* (Baltimore: Johns Hopkins University Press, 2004), 74–78.

[69]For further discussion of this theme, see Lopez, *Separatist Christianity*.

[70]Frend, *Martyrdom and Persecution in the Early Church*, 200. On the reference to the soldiers, see Ignatius, *Romans* 5.1.

[71]Ignatius, *Romans* 7.8, in Staniforth, *Early Christian Writings*, 87, altered.

almost definitely an allusion to Jesus' words in John 7:37–39 that liken the
Holy Spirit to "rivers of living water."[72] It is the Spirit, therefore, who speaks
within Ignatius, "Come to the Father." The Spirit speaks thus from within
a context of crucifixion: the death of Ignatius's "earthly longings," according to Maxwell Staniforth's translation cited above.[73] This phrase "earthly
longings" is literally "my love."[74] In the century following Ignatius, the great
Alexandrian exegete Origen initiated a long tradition of interpretation of
this Ignatian text when he remarked that "one of the saints, by name Ignatius, said of Christ, 'My Love is crucified.'"[75] Origen goes on to say that he
finds it odd that Ignatius uses the term erōs for Christ, but he states that he
is unwilling to censure him for such. However, over and above the fact that
the term erōs is not used in the New Testament at all, which I do not think
is very significant, the context of Ignatius's statement seems to demand that
it be understood as "earthly longings." The use of the conjunction and places
the phrase "earthly longings" on the same level as the clause "in me there is
left no spark of desire for mundane things."[76] In other words, the "living
water," the Spirit, has quenched the fire of "earthly passion" and is exhorting
Ignatius to "come to the Father."[77] Thus, the Spirit is leading Ignatius to the
Father by way of martyrdom, and his leading entails a death to all earthly
longings. This passage reflects both a keen understanding of the opposition
of the Spirit to "earthly longings"[78] and the awareness that martyrdom is, in
a sense, a gift of the Spirit.

---

[72]See also the link of the Spirit and water in Rev. 22:1–2, 17. See the comments of Schoedel, *Ignatius of Antioch*, 185; Henning Paulsen, *Die Briefe des Ignatius von Antiochia und der Brief des Polykarp von Smyrna* (Tübingen: Mohr Siebeck, 1985), 77.

[73]Similarly, Schoedel, *Ignatius of Antioch*, 181: "My longing."

[74]Thus J. H. Srawley, *The Epistles of St. Ignatius Bishop of Antioch*, 3rd ed. (London: Society for Pro-moting Christian Knowledge, 1919), 78; Paulsen, *Die Briefe des Ignatius von Antiochia*, 76: "Meine Liebe."

[75]*Commentary on the Song of Songs*, prologue 2, in *Origen: The Song of Songs Commentary and Homilies*, trans. R. P. Lawson, Ancient Christian Writers 26 (Westminster, MD: Newman, 1957), 35. For another much later example, see Samuel Pearce, "Lines written on the words of Ignatius, 'My Love Is Crucified,'" in Andrew Fuller, *Memoirs of the Rev. Samuel Pearce, A.M.*, ed. W. H. Pearce (London: G. Wightman, 1831), 223–25. Pearce (1766–1799), an English Calvinistic Baptist pastor, clearly understands Ignatius's words to be a reference to Christ. On Origen, see below, chapter 4.

[76]I am indebted to a good friend, Dr. Benjamin Hegeman of SIM, who is now based in Houghton, New York, for this point.

[77]P. Th. Camelot, trans., *Ignace d'Antioche, Polycarpe de Smyrne: Lettres, Martyre de Polycarpe*, 3rd ed. (Paris: Les Éditions du Cerf, 1958), 134–35n1; Brown, *Gospel and Ignatius of Antioch*, 109.

[78]Similarly J. B. Lightfoot translates this phrase by "my earthly passion has been crucified," in *The Apostolic Fathers: Clement, Ignatius, and Polycarp*, 2nd ed. (repr., Grand Rapids: Baker, 1981), 2/2:222. See also the comments of Castelli, *Martyrdom and Memory*, 81, 83.

Martyrdom as a Gift of the Spirit

While the church disapproved of people volunteering to be martyrs,[79] there are a number of Christian texts from the second century that display the awareness that martyrdom was a calling, a gift (*charisma*), from the Spirit that he would use to build up the body of Christ. Ignatius's letter to the Romans is certainly a key passage in this regard. Another would be a statement made by the Latin-speaking editor of the prison diary of the early third-century martyr Vibia Perpetua. Arrested in Carthage and subsequently martyred in that city along with a number of other Christians in the spring of 203, Perpetua kept a diary while in prison. A later editor—some have suggested the North African author Tertullian—then published it and the diary from the hand of another martyr, Saturus, with an editorial introduction and conclusion. In the introduction we read the following:

> The deeds recounted about the faith in ancient times were a proof of God's favour and achieved the spiritual strengthening of men as well; and they were set forth in writing precisely that honour might be rendered to God and comfort to men by the recollection of the past through the written word. Should not then more recent examples be set down that contribute equally to both ends? For indeed these too will one day become ancient and needful for the ages to come, even though in our own day they may enjoy less prestige because of the prior claim of antiquity.
>
> Let those then who would restrict the power of the one Spirit to times and seasons look to this: the more recent events should be considered the greater, being later than those of old, and this is a consequence of the extraordinary graces promised for the last stage of time. For "in the last days, God declares, I will pour out my Spirit upon all flesh and their sons and daughter shall prophesy and on my menservants and my maidservants I will pour my Spirit, and the young shall see visions and the old men shall dream dreams." So too we hold in honour and acknowledge not only new prophecies but new visions as well, according to the promise. And we consider all the other functions of the Holy Spirit as intended for the good of the Church; for the same Spirit has been sent to distribute all his gifts to all, as the Lord apportions to everyone.[80]

---

[79] *The Martyrdom of Polycarp* 4.

[80] *The Martyrdom of Saints Perpetua and Felicitas* 1.1–5, in *The Acts of the Christian Martyrs*, trans. Herbert Musurillo (Oxford: Clarendon, 1972), 107. For a discussion of this account, see especially Brent D. Shaw, "The Passion of Perpetua," *Past and Present* 139 (May 1993): 3–45.

Some have argued that this text emanates from circles influenced by the claims of Montanism, a late second-century renewal movement that argued for new revelations from God, especially with regard to moral questions.[81] Be this as it may, it clearly includes Christian martyrdom among the "functions of the Holy Spirit . . . intended for the good of the Church."

If one were to enquire as to what biblical references inform this understanding of martyrdom, a passage like 1 Corinthians 13:1–3 immediately springs to mind. There the apostle Paul argues that gifts of the Spirit—such as glossolalia and prophecy—that are used without the motive power of love, are ultimately without value. Among the gifts he mentions is the willing surrender of one's life by fire, which clearly implies that in Paul's mind martyrdom is to be ranked among the *charismata*, the gifts of the Holy Spirit.

Martyrdom and Being a Disciple

In an important study of Ignatius as martyr and Christian disciple, Daniel N. McNamara notes that within Ignatius's letters the bishop of Antioch speaks of "being a disciple" in two different ways. First, he expresses the hope that he will "be found a disciple" in his confrontation with death as a martyr. By this McNamara understands Ignatius to be saying that "he hoped that his final confrontation with death would be found consistent with his profession of faith in Christ." In a second understanding of what it means to be a Christian disciple, the emphasis is placed on the devotion of the Christian to the Lord Jesus.[82]

For Ignatius, martyrdom is the clearest way to express his personal devotion to Christ and his rejection of the world. But he is quite aware that there are other ways to journey. For example, his urging of the believers in Rome to express their devotion to Christ by allowing him to die as a martyr clearly indicates an awareness that his path of discipleship and theirs are not identical. Although Ignatius might see martyrdom as the straighter road upon which he must travel, he is not denying the fact that there are other paths that other disciples may travel.[83] In this regard, it is vital to note that he does not exhort any of the believers in Rome, nor for that matter any of his other

---

[81]On Montanism, see especially Ronald E. Heine, *The Montanist Oracles and Testimonia*, Patristic Monograph Series 14 (Macon, GA: Mercer University Press, 1989); and William Tabbernee, *Prophets and Gravestones: An Imaginative History of Montanists and Other Early Christians* (Peabody, MA: Hendrickson, 2009).

[82]Daniel N. McNamara, "Ignatius of Antioch on His Death: Discipleship, Sacrifice, Imitation" (PhD diss., McMaster University, 1977), 247.

[83]Corwin, *St. Ignatius and Christianity in Antioch*, 254–55.

correspondents, to join him as a martyr. He obviously does not see martyrdom as being essential to discipleship.[84]

Martyrdom and the Defense of the Faith

A final aspect of Ignatius's thinking about his martyrdom is the way that he believes it forms a bulwark against a species of false teaching that threatened the unity of at least a couple of the churches to which he was writing, namely, those in Smyrna and in Tralles. Present even during the days of the apostles,[85] the proponents of this perspective, known as Docetism, denied the death of Christ and asserted that Christ's "sufferings were not genuine."[86] Ignatius uses what was becoming a technical word to describe these theological opponents of core Christian teaching: they have embraced "heresy" (hairesis).[87] Moreover, according to Ignatius, those who have embraced this false teaching do not live godly lives, for they have broken with the church, refusing to attend the Lord's Table or to pray together with the church.[88] While Docetism was not part and parcel of every variant of second-century heresy, it can be found in a goodly variety of heretical documents from that period. In the second-century text *The Letter of Peter to Philip*, for example, it is asserted that "Jesus is a stranger to ... suffering." In another text of the same ilk, the *First Apocalypse of James*, a statement is attributed to Christ in which he affirms, "Never have I suffered in any way."[89]

Now, in the letter to the church at Smyrna Ignatius makes a powerful connection between his own death and that of Christ. He writes that Christ was "truly pierced by nails in his human flesh" and "truly suffered." It is thus necessary to confess, over against the heretics, that "his Passion was no unreal illusion."[90] Nor was Christ's physical resurrection an illusion. "For my own part," Ignatius declares, "I know and believe that he was in actual human flesh, even after his resurrection." Ignatius finds proof for this declaration in

---

[84]Frend, *Martyrdom and Persecution in the Early Church*, 198. See also, in this regard, Ignatius's exhortation to Polycarp in *Polycarp* 2.

[85]See, for example, in the New Testament: 1 John 4:1–3; 2 John 7–11.

[86]Ignatius, *Trallians* 9–11.

[87]See Ignatius, *Trallians* 6.1. He also uses the term "teaching falsehood" (*heterodoxountas*) with regard to this perspective (Ignatius, *Smyrnaeans* 6.2). It is interesting that Ignatius is the only second-century Christian author to use this term. See Brown, *The Gospel and Ignatius of Antioch*, 174–75.

[88]Ignatius, *Smyrnaeans* 6–7.

[89]Both texts cited by Guy G. Stroumsa, "Christ's Laughter: Docetic Origins Reconsidered," *Journal of Early Christian Studies* 12 (2004): 272.

[90]Ignatius, *Smyrnaeans* 1.2–2, in Staniforth, *Early Christian Writings*, 101, altered.

the resurrection accounts in Luke 24, where Christ appeared to his disciples, challenged their unbelief, and urged them to eat and drink with him.[91]

If the Docetists were correct and all of the Lord Jesus' life were only an illusion, then, Ignatius declares with biting sarcasm, "these chains of mine must be illusory too!"[92] From the point of view of Docetism, if Christ did not really suffer, it was meaningless for any of his disciples to take such a pathway. Martyrdom was thus not a distinctive characteristic of the Docetist communities. A number of second-century authors after Ignatius indeed note the absence of martyrs among such communities.[93] But Christ's suffering was real and this validated the physical suffering of his people. Ignatius continues:

> To what end have I given myself up to perish by fire or sword or savage beasts? Simply because when I am close to the sword I am close to God, and when I am surrounded by the lions, I am surrounded by God. But it is only in the name of Jesus Christ, and for the sake of sharing his sufferings, that I could face all this; for he, the perfect Man, gives me strength to do so.[94]

Ignatius's martyrdom was thus a powerful defense of the saving reality of the incarnation and crucifixion. In suffering a violent death, Ignatius was confessing that his Lord had also actually suffered a violent demise, and through it brought salvation to dying humanity. So important was that confession, so central was it to Christian orthodoxy, that it was worth dying for. And in our day, when Christians are being martyred around the globe, Ignatius's confession should not be forgotten.

---

[91]Ignatius, *Smyrnaeans* 3.1–2, in Staniforth, *Early Christian Writings*, 101. On the Docetists at Smyrna, see also Sumney, "The Opponents of Ignatius of Antioch," 349–53; Isacson, *To Each Their Own Letter*, 158–79.

[92]*Smyrnaeans* 4.2, in Staniforth, *Early Christian Writings*, 102. See also *Trallians* 9–10.

[93]See the references in Pagels, "Gnostic and Orthodox Views of Christ's Passion," 265–71. It needs noting that there were a few Gnostics who appear to have affirmed Christ's bodily sufferings and thus the value of martyrdom: see ibid., passim; Heikki Räisänen, "Marcion," in *A Companion to Second-Century Christian "Heretics,"* ed. Antii Marjanen and Petri Luomanen (Leiden: E. J. Brill, 2005), 100–124.

[94]*Smyrnaeans* 4.2, in Staniforth, *Early Christian Writings*, 102.

Chapter 3

SHARING THE TRUTH

The Letter to Diognetus

. . . we are in him who is true, in his Son Jesus Christ.
He is the true God and eternal life.

1 JOHN 5:20

y and large, the writings of the New Testament era as well as those from the period immediately following, the works of the so-called apostolic fathers, are concerned with establishing the faith and discipline of Christian communities. They are works that generally address those within the fold of Christianity. After AD 150, though, there is a noticeable shift in the orientation of Christian literature. There is now a significant stress on what we call apologetics, that is, the presentation of reasons for holding to the Christian faith, the attempt to answer the ridicule and objections of unbelievers, and the attack on alternative worldviews in the Graeco-Roman world, exposing their inadequacies and problems for belief.

One of the most attractive of these second-century apologies is the *Letter to Diognetus*, a spirited and stirring defense of the truth of the Christian

A good portion of this chapter has appeared in chapter 1 of my *Defence of the Truth: Contending for the Truth Yesterday and Today* (Darlington, UK: Evangelical Press, 2004). Used by permission.

worldview.[1] In fact, Avery Dulles, in his *History of Apologetics*, describes it as "the pearl of early Christian apologetics."[2] It stems from the joyous faith of a man who stands amazed at the revelation of God's love in his Son and who is seeking to persuade a Graeco-Roman pagan by the name of Diognetus to make a commitment to the Christian faith.

As to who wrote this marvelous Christian treatise—it is really more a treatise than a letter—we do not know. From its elegant Greek it can be observed that "the author was a Christian of cultured mind, with a Classical training, who was possessed of considerable literary skill and style."[3] Nor is the identity of Diognetus, the recipient, known, though some have speculated he may have been one of the tutors of the philosopher-emperor Marcus Aurelius (r. 161–180).[4] And beyond the fact that this masterful apologetic was written within the bounds of the Roman Empire, probably in the eastern portion of the empire, the exact geographical location of its author is also unknown. However, we do have some idea of its date. There is evidence within the text that would place it in the final quarter of the second century.[5]

Before we look more closely at its reasoned defense of Christianity, a word should be said about the intriguing circumstances by which we have come to possess this document. We owe our knowledge of the text to a single thirteenth- or fourteenth-century manuscript that was discovered in Constantinople in 1436. An Italian scholar by the name of Thomas of Arezzo happened upon it in a fish shop where it lay under a pile of wrap-

---

[1]For studies of the *Letter to Diognetus*, see especially Henry G. Meecham, *The Epistle to Diognetus: The Greek Text with Introduction, Translation and Notes* (Manchester: Manchester University Press, 1949); L. W. Barnard, "The Enigma of the Epistle to Diognetus," in *Studies in the Apostolic Fathers and Their Background* (Oxford: Basil Blackwell, 1966), 165–73; Joseph T. Lienhard, "The Christology of the Epistle to Diognetus," *Vigiliae Christianae* 24 (1970): 280–89; A. L. Townsley, "Notes for an Interpretation of the Epistle to Diognetus," *Rivista di studi classici* 24 (1976): 5–20; Charles E. Hill, *From the Lost Teaching of Polycarp: Identifying Irenaeus' Apostolic Presbyter and the Author of* Ad Diognetum, Wissenschaftliche Untersuchungen zum Neuen Testament 186 (Tübingen: Mohr Siebeck, 2006); Paul Foster, "The Epistle to Diognetus," *The Expository Times* 118 (2007): 162–68.
[2]*A History of Apologetics* (New York: Corpus Instrumentorum; Philadelphia: Westminster Press, 1971), 28.
[3]Barnard, "Epistle to Diognetus," 172. See also the comments of J. G. O'Neill, "The Epistle to Diognetus," *The Irish Ecclesiastical Record* 85 (1956): 93. For a list of possible authors, see Barnard, "Epistle to Diognetus," 171–72. Charles E. Hill has recently argued, unconvincingly to this author, that Polycarp of Smyrna wrote the *Letter to Diognetus*. See Hill, *From the Lost Teaching of Polycarp*.
[4]See the discussion of Dulles, *History of Apologetics*, 28–29.
[5]For this dating, see Robert M. Grant, *Greek Apologists of the Second Century* (Philadelphia: Westminster Press, 1988), 178–79. W. S. Walford, *Epistle to Diognetus* (London: James Nisbet, 1908), 7–9, and Barnard, "Epistle to Diognetus," 172–73, would date it no later than 140.

ping paper. There is little doubt that it would have been used to wrap up a sale if the scholar had not rescued it! According to the scribe who copied this manuscript, he took it from a very old exemplar. The German historian Adolf von Harnack (1851–1930) believed this exemplar was a sixth- or seventh-century document.[6] At some point the manuscript discovered in the Constantinople fish shop came into the hands of the German scholar Johannes Reuchlin (1455–1522), the granduncle of the Lutheran Reformer Philipp Melanchthon (1497–1560), and at least five copies of it were made.[7] Eventually the manuscript found a home in the university library of Strasbourg. It was good that copies of it were made, for on August 24, 1870, the library was burned to the ground as Prussian artillery pounded the city during the Franco-Prussian war. It needs noting that the line of transmission of this early Christian apology is typical of all of the books from the ancient world: our knowledge of them usually rests on a few textual witnesses.[8] The one exception is the Scriptures.

One further aspect of the text of the treatise should be mentioned. There are three major gaps in the text: at 7.7, 10.1, and 10.8.[9] The last of these gaps is the most serious for it comes right at the end of the treatise, and so we do not know how the text actually ends. In our copies of this text there are two further chapters, *Diognetus* 11–12, but they are not part of the apology. Rather, they are a homily that celebrates the impact of the living Word, the Son of God, in the life of the church and that has, in the course of time, become attached to the apologetic work. It is quite possible that the author of both sections of *Diognetus* is one and the same, which would easily explain this situation.

The Introduction

In the first chapter of the treatise, the author notes that Diognetus is interested in learning about the Christian faith. In fact, he has three specific questions that he wants answered:

> I have noticed, most excellent Diognetus, the deep interest you have been showing in Christianity, and the close and careful inquiries you have been

[6]O'Neill, "Epistle to Diognetus," 93–94.

[7]Ibid., 94.

[8]Simon Price and Peter Thoneman, *The Birth of Classical Europe: A History from Troy to Augustine*, The Penguin History of Europe 1 (London: Allen Lane, 2010), 317–18.

[9]Reference to the *Letter to Diognetus* is according to chapter and verse. I am following the chapter and verse divisions of Meecham, *Epistle to Diognetus*.

making about it. You would like to know what God Christians believe in, and what sort of worship they practice which enables them to set so little store by this world and even to make light of death itself—since they reject the deities revered by the Greeks no less than they disclaim the superstitions professed by the Jews. You are curious, too, about the warm fraternal affection they all feel for one another. Also, you are puzzled as to why this new race of men, or at least this novel manner of life, has only come into our lives recently, instead of much earlier.[10]

The first question is basically an inquiry about who is the Christian God. It is rooted in the fact that the Greeks and Romans regularly accused the early Christians of being atheists, since they refused to worship the Greek and Roman gods. The second question—why do Christians love each other the way they do—is especially noteworthy. Many pagans were struck by the way that the ancient church was a community of love, something very different from their own experience of social relationships. The final question has its basis in the Greek and Roman reverence for antiquity.[11] What was true had to be ancient. If it was recent, it was suspect.[12] If Christianity was true, why had the culture's ancients not known of it? The recent origin of Christianity thus posed a major stumbling block for acceptance of its truth claims.[13]

It is fascinating to note the final sentence of this opening section of the treatise. "I pray God," the Christian author says, "the Author of both our speech and hearing, to grant me such use of my tongue that you may derive the fullest benefit from listening to me, and to you such use of your ears that I may have no cause to regret having spoken."[14] This is nothing less than a prayer for Diognetus's conversion. In other words, the author clearly assumes that the embrace of Christian truth cannot come from reason alone. God must give Diognetus the ability "to hear" the truth.

---

[10]*Letter to Diognetus* 1, in *Early Christian Writings*, trans. Maxwell Staniforth (1968; repr. Harmondsworth, UK: Penguin, 1987), 142, altered. There are various translations of the *Letter to Diognetus*. Staniforth's is one of the most readable. Hereafter this translation will be cited as Staniforth, *Early Christian Writings*.

[11]See Price and Thoneman, *Birth of Classical Europe*, passim.

[12]Stephen Benko, *Pagan Rome and the Early Christians* (Bloomington: Indiana University Press, 1984), 21–22; Wolfram Kinzig, "The Idea of Progress in the Early Church until the Age of Constantine," in *Studia Patristica*, ed. Elizabeth A. Livingstone (Louvain: Peeters, 1993), 24:123–25.

[13]See also Theophilus of Antioch, *To Autolycus* 3.4 for this charge of novelty.

[14]*Letter to Diognetus* 1, in Staniforth, *Early Christian Writings*, 142.

Incidentally, this sentence also tells us something of the importance placed upon speech in Graeco-Roman society. The author writes not of "writing and reading" but of "speech and hearing." This treatise, like many of the texts of the ancient world, including those of the New Testament, would have been dictated to a scribe. And when it was received, the recipient would have read it aloud, not silently as we would today. Not surprisingly, there was a profound preference for the spoken word over the written word in the surrounding culture, although this was not true of the ancient church generally.[15] There is a well-known passage in the *Confessions* of the great North African theologian Augustine in which he recounts his observation of the reading habits of the northern Italian bishop Ambrose, who was instrumental in his conversion. What Augustine found most striking was the fact that Ambrose read silently to himself. It was obvious to a bystander that the bishop was reading, but he was doing it in a way quite foreign to the mores of the ancient world.[16] Normally when one read, one pronounced the words out loud.

The Folly of Graeco-Roman Idolatry

The first three sections of the letter after the opening chapter contain a vigorous attack on both Graeco-Roman paganism and Judaism. The former is attacked for it engages in the folly of worshipping the products of human imagination and technology (2.1–10). The latter, the author admits, worships the true God, but with a wrong understanding, for the Jews think God stands in need of their sacrifices (3.3–5). The frontal attack made upon Graeco-Roman paganism is particularly instructive about the way in which the second-century church went about defending its faith in a pluralistic culture.

The Greeks and Romans were unashamedly polytheistic. Their universe was peopled with innumerable gods and divine spirits. Forests and fields, homes and places of employment, earth and sky and water were thought to be filled with these beings. The apostle Paul mentions this popular understanding of the universe in 1 Corinthians 8:5 when he states that the surrounding Greek and Roman culture knew of "many 'gods' and many 'lords'" in heaven

---

[15] See Loveday Alexander, "The Living Voice: Scepticism towards the Written Word in Early Christian and in Graeco-Roman Texts," in *The Bible in Three Dimensions: Essays in Celebration of Forty Years of Biblical Studies in the University of Sheffield*, ed. David J. A. Clines, Stephen E. Fowl, and Stanley E. Porter, Journal for the Study of the Old Testament Supplement Series 87 (Sheffield: Sheffield Academic, 1990), 221–47.

[16] Augustine, *Confessions* 6.3.3.

and on earth. But, the apostle goes on in the following verse, whatever his Greek and Roman contemporaries might believe, he and his fellow Christians were assured that there was but "one God, the Father" and "one Lord, Jesus Christ." As for the Greek and Roman gods, the ancient church recognized that they have, in Paul's words, "no real existence" (1 Cor. 8:4). Undoubtedly they "existed" for those who worshipped them, but from the standpoint of reality they simply did not exist. They were, as Paul says in his speech on Mars Hill, a classic defense of the Christian perspective on life, "formed by the art and imagination of man" (Acts 17:29).

Drawing upon this monotheistic foundation and critique of Graeco-Roman idolatry, the author of the *Letter to Diognetus* seeks first to show Diognetus that the gods and goddesses whom he worships are nothing more than the products of human technology.

> Take a good look—with your intelligence, not just with your eyes—at the forms and substances of those objects which you call gods and hold to be divine. Is this one here, for instance, anything other than a block of stone, identical in kind with the flagstones we tread under our feet? Is not that one there made out of brass, of no finer quality than the common utensils that are manufactured for our everyday use? A third of wood, already rotting into decay? A fourth of silver, needing someone to keep an eye on it all the time for fear of thieves? A fifth of iron, pitted all over with rust, and a sixth of no better-looking earthenware than the articles they turn out for the humblest domestic purposes? Is not every single one of these made of materials that are perishable? Was not one made by the stonecutter, another by a brass-founder, a third by a silversmith, a fourth by a potter? And up to the moment when the skill of those craftsmen gave them their present forms, was it not just as practicable—indeed, is it not just as practicable even now—for every one of them to have been made into something quite different? . . . In a word, are they not, one and all, nothing but dumb, blind, lifeless things, without sense, without movement, rotting and decaying?
>
> Do you really call these things gods, and really do service to them? Yes, indeed you do; you worship them—and you end up by becoming like them. Is it not because we Christians refuse to acknowledge their divinity that you dislike us so?[17]

---

[17] *Letter to Diognetus* 2.1b–6, in Staniforth, *Early Christian Writings*, 142–43, altered.

This passage not only is indebted to the passages from the apostle Paul that
we have noted above. It also goes back to texts in the Old Testament, such as
Jeremiah 10:3–10, that ridicule the foolishness of the idolatry of the pagan
nations around Israel.[18]

The author then seeks to reason with his pagan correspondent. By rejecting their society's idolatry, Christians have drawn upon themselves the oppro-
brium of their fellow citizens (2.6). But, in fact, are not those who worship
these gods and goddesses more disrespectful of them?

> It is surely a mockery and an affront to them that, so long as these venerated
> deities are only made of stone or pottery, you leave them quite unprotected,
> but when they are silver or gold, then you lock them up every night, and
> post watchmen over them all day, in case they might be stolen. And if they
> are really endowed with sense, the sort of honours you pay to them must
> be more of a humiliation than a tribute; and if they are not, then you are
> making nonsense of them when you adore them with the blood and fat of
> your sacrifices.[19]

The author notes that he could say a lot more about the folly of Graeco-
Roman religious rites and views, but he believes one final comment will
suffice: "Christians are not in bondage to such gods" (2.10). To understand
fully this final comment one must bear in mind the apostle Paul's discussion
in 1 Corinthians of the idolatry of his day. Paul, as we have seen, maintained
first of all that the Greek and Roman gods and goddesses had no objective
reality. Yet, he went on to argue, this did not mean that pagan religion was
harmless. In fact, it was "the locus of demonic activity, and . . . to worship
such 'gods' is in fact to fellowship with demons" (see 1 Cor. 10:19–20).[20]
These demonic powers used traditional Greek and Roman religion with its
various rites and myths as so many masks to ensnare men and women and
so bring them into a state of bondage.[21] Conversion to Christianity then
not only meant coming to the realization that Graeco-Roman religion was

---

[18]See also the critique of idolatry in extrabiblical Jewish literature, for instance, *The Wisdom of Solomon*
13.10–15.17. It should be noted that there was also a long philosophical tradition among the Greeks
that ridiculed the superstitions of polytheism. See Dulles, *History of Apologetics*, 23.

[19]*Letter to Diognetus* 2.7–8, in Staniforth, *Early Christian Writings*, 143.

[20]Gordon D. Fee, *The First Epistle to the Corinthians* (Grand Rapids: Eerdmans, 1987), 370.

[21]Peter Brown, *The Rise of Western Christendom: Triumph and Diversity AD 200–1000* (Oxford: Blackwell, 1996), 27.

a "grand illusion,"[22] but also spelled freedom from the tyranny of numerous demonic powers.

The True Maker of the Universe and His Beloved Son

A good defense of the Christian faith not only displays the problems with rival worldviews, but also sets forth how Christians view the world. Thus, after the author of this second-century apology has differentiated Christian worship from that of Judaism (3.1–4.6) and discussed the ways in which the Christian lifestyle is at once identical to and yet radically different from that of their pagan neighbors (5.1–6.10),[23] he turns to answer Diognetus's first question: who is the God in whom Christians trust?

The writer begins by indicating that the Christian concept of God is not the product of human thought or philosophy. He has already mentioned this fact in chapter 5: "The doctrine they [i.e., Christians] profess is not the invention of busy human minds and brains, nor are they, like some, adherents of this or that school of human thought" (5.3). Now, in chapter 7, he gives a much fuller statement.

> As I said before, it is not an earthly discovery that has been entrusted to them [i.e., Christians]. The thing they guard so jealously is no product of mortal thinking, and what has been committed to them is the stewardship of no human mysteries. The Almighty himself, the Creator of the universe, the God whom no eye can discern, has sent down his very own Truth from heaven, his own holy and incomprehensible Word, to plant it among men and ground it in their hearts.[24]

Here the author affirms unequivocally that Christian truth is ultimately not a matter of mere human reason or religious speculation. Rather, it is rooted in God's revelation of himself. The writer here assumes a key principle for Patristic theologians: ultimately only God can reveal God, and we can know nothing about God unless he reveals himself.

The same point is made yet a third time in 8.1–5.

> Before his [i.e., Christ's] advent, who among mankind had any notion at all of what God is? Or do you accept the vapid and ludicrous suggestions

---

[22]This description is that of ibid.

[23]For a discussion of chapter 5, see Bruce Fawcett, "Similar yet Unique: Christians as Described in the *Letter to Diognetus* 5," *The Baptist Review of Theology* 6, no. 1 (Spring 1996): 23–27.

[24]*Letter to Diognetus* 7.1–2, in Staniforth, *Early Christian Writings*, 146, altered.

of your own pretentious philosophers?—some of whom assure us that God is Fire (thus giving the name of God to what they will surely come to one day themselves!), some that he is Water, and others one of the other various elements of his creation. If any of those ideas were admissible, there would be no reason why anything else in the world could not be declared to be God. Assertions of that sort are no more than the hocus-pocus, the "hey, presto!," of professional illusionists, for no man living has ever seen him or known him; it is he himself who has given us the revelation of himself.[25]

Two philosophical speculations about the nature of God are here mentioned and rejected, both of them from the earliest period of Greek philosophy. The first, the assertion that God is fire, comes from the philosopher Heraclitus of Ephesus (fl. 500 BC), who could also make the pantheistic statement: "God is day and night, summer and winter, war and peace, fullness and want." The declaration that God is water appears to be a reference to the Ionian thinker Thales (fl. 580–540 BC), the father of Greek philosophy. Unlike some of his Christian contemporaries, notably Justin Martyr, who regarded Greek philosophical thought as playing an important, albeit subordinate, role in preparing Graeco-Roman civilization for the gospel, the writer of this letter flatly asserts the opposite. In the words of H. G. Meecham, "All such strivings after God are discredited."[26] As the above-quoted text asserts, God was unknown before he revealed himself.

His revelation of himself, the author of this treatise further maintains, was made through the incarnation of his Son. God has not, he writes,

sent to mankind some servant of his, some angel or prince. . . . It is no other than the universal Artificer and Maker himself, by whose agency God made the heavens and set the seas their bounds; . . . by whom the sun is assigned the limits of his course by day, and at whose command by night the obedient moon unveils her beams, and each compliant star follows circling in her train. Ordainer, Disposer, and Ruler of all things is he; of heaven and all that heaven holds, of earth and all that is in earth, of sea and every creature therein; of fires, air and the abyss; of things above, and things below, and things in the midst. Such was the Messenger God sent to men.[27]

---

[25] *Letter to Diognetus* 8.1–5, in Staniforth, *Early Christian Writings*, 146–47, altered.

[26] "The Theology of the Epistle to Diognetus," *The Expository Times* 54 (1942–1943): 98.

[27] *Letter to Diognetus* 7.2, in Staniforth, *Early Christian Writings*, 146, altered.

It is noteworthy that the author of this treatise does not go into God's revelation of himself prior to the incarnation of Christ. Yet, this is central to the New Testament witness to Christ. The God who spoke in the past and revealed himself through his servants, the prophets, is now speaking through his Son. As we read in Hebrews 1:1–2, "God, who at various times and in various ways spoke in time past to the fathers by the prophets, has in these last days spoken to us by His Son" (NKJV). Failure to take into account God's revelation of himself in the Old Testament era will cause problems for the author of this treatise when he comes to answer Diognetus's question concerning the antiquity of Christianity. But we will come back to this later.

Christianity, then, is ultimately not a human attempt to find God, whether by philosophical speculation or by religious ritual. Rather, it is founded on God's revelation of himself, and that in a person, his Son. Although the personal name of the incarnate Son, Jesus, is not mentioned in this treatise as a whole, there is no doubt that this is the person of whom the author writes so eloquently in the above-cited passage. The Son does not belong to the order of creation, as is clear from the text from 7.2 that is quoted above. In this passage, the Son's dominion over the entirety of nature, and by implication his deity, is trumpeted forth.

The Son, by whom God made the heavens and the earth and all that they contain,[28] was sent to reveal God. "As a king sending his royal son," the author declares, "so sent he him; as God he sent him; as Man to men he sent him" (7.2). These words reveal a high doctrine of Christ. Who is this One whom God sent to reveal himself? Well, he is "a son." He is sent "as God." When he called men to repentance and faith, it was God who was calling. As L. B. Radford comments, "He is God so truly that His coming can be described as the coming of God."[29]

A reasoned defense of the Christian faith cannot, therefore, leave out of consideration the person of Christ. Indeed, it is upon his uniqueness and deity that Christianity hangs. Now, some have argued that the *Letter to Diognetus* cannot be described as having a theology and that the author purposely avoids "dogmatic precision."[30] But this section of the treatise can

---

[28]For biblical attestation of this same truth, see John 1:3, 10; Col. 1:16; Heb. 1:2.

[29]*The Epistle to Diognetus* (London, 1908), 39. See also Lienhard, "Christology of the Epistle to Diognetus," 288.

[30]Craig Steven Wansink, "*Epistula ad Diognetum*: A School Exercise in the Use of Protreptic," in *Church Divinity 1986*, ed. John H. Morgan (Bristol, IN: Wyndham Hall, 1986), 97–109.

hardly be described as atheological, nor can the discussion on the cross that now follows.

The Antiquity of Christianity and the Cross

This discussion of the way in which God has revealed himself opens the way for the author to provide an answer to what would have been a basic question for most peoples in the Roman Empire, whether Jew, Greek, or Roman—the last of the questions mentioned in the first chapter of the treatise: "Why has this new race of men, or at least this novel manner of living, only come into our lives recently, instead of much earlier?" It was axiomatic among the ancients that what was true was old, and what was new was questionable and probably false. This raised an obvious problem for those seeking to convince men and women of the truth claims of Christianity, for Christianity took its rise from the appearance of Christ. The standard answer among Christian apologists was that the Old Testament era predicted the coming of Christ. Seen in this light, Christian truth had a much better claim to antiquity than either Greek or Roman thought, neither of which was over a millennium old.

The *Letter to Diognetus*, however, does not take this approach. Earlier, in the sections dealing with Judaism, the author had taken such a hard stance against Judaism (3–4) that the impression is given that Judaism was of no value at all, not even as a forerunner of Christianity. Thus, the author is forced to argue that although God conceived the design of sending his Son to redeem humanity, at first he told it to nobody but the Son. Then, when men and women had shown by their "unruly instincts and . . . sensuality and lust" that they were both "unworthy to achieve life" and "unable to enter into the kingdom of God by [their] own power," God sent forth his Son.[31]

Even though this argument as it stands, without any hint of the Old Testament period of preparation, is probably the only major weakness of the letter, it does provide yet another support for embracing the Christian faith. The author has argued that God revealed his plan of salvation to none but his "beloved Son" until men realized their utter and complete inability to gain heaven by their own strength. Then, when men were conscious of their sin and the impending judgment, God did the following:

---

[31]*Letter to Diognetus* 8.9–9.2, in Staniforth, *Early Christian Writings*, 147, altered.

Instead of hating us and rejecting us and remembering our wickednesses against us, he showed how long-suffering he is. He bore with us, and in pity he took our sins upon himself and gave his own Son as a ransom for us—the Holy for the wicked, the Sinless for sinners, the Just for the unjust, the Incorruptible for the corruptible, the Immortal for the mortal. For was there, indeed, anything except his righteousness that could have availed to cover our sins? In whom could we, in our lawlessness and ungodliness, have been made holy, but in the Son of God alone? O sweet exchange! O unsearchable working! O benefits unhoped for!—that the wickedness of multitudes should thus be hidden in the One righteous, and the righteousness of One should justify the countless wicked!

In times past, he convinced us that our human nature by itself lacked the power of attaining to life; today, he reveals to us a Saviour who has power to save even the powerless. The purpose behind both of these acts is that we should believe in his goodness, and should look on him as our Nourisher, Father, Teacher, Counsellor, Healer, Wisdom, Light, Honour, Glory, Power, and Life, and have no anxiety about our clothing or our food.[32]

The use of the term *ransom* at the head of this passage recalls Mark 10:45 ("the Son of Man came not to be served but to serve, and to give his life as a ransom for many"), where *ransom* bears all of the force of its meaning as a payment that is substitutionary in character.[33] Here, in the *Letter to Diognetus* this substitutionary motif is also in view in the letter's use of the term *ransom*, as the subsequent clauses of this text clearly display. Five dialectical ways are employed to express this act of substitution, one of which—"the Righteous One for the unrighteous"—almost exactly reproduces a phrase from 1 Peter 3:18. What is highlighted in this dialectic are the twin soteriological themes of the Son's utter sinlessness and humanity's radical depravity, a dialectic that recalls the rich Pauline theology of salvation as found in passages like Romans 5:6–10.

This is a truly marvelous text, as the author, overwhelmed by what took place at the cross, is lost in rapture, awe, and praise. Here, as so often happens in the writings of Paul, theology gives way to doxology. Yet, the doxological nature of this passage should not lead us to overlook the way that it also contributed to the author's defense of the Christian worldview. Why should the truth claims of Christianity be weighed seriously? Unlike

---

[32]*Letter to Diognetus* 9.2–5, in Staniforth, *Early Christian Writings*, 147–48, altered.

[33]Leon Morris, *The Apostolic Preaching of the Cross*, 3rd. ed. (London: Tyndale, 1965), 33–38.

other religions, Christianity deals decisively with the fundamental human problem—the problem of human sin. The renowned authority on early church history Henry Chadwick puts this point well when he states that one of the major reasons for the growth of the church was the fact that the gospel it preached "spoke of divine grace in Christ, the remission of sins and the conquest of evil powers for the sick soul, tired of living and scared of dying, seeking for an assurance of immortality."[34] This passage is also a good reminder that Christian apologetics, though using reason, need not be dry and lifeless. It can, indeed must, speak to the heart as well as to the mind.

The upshot of being enfolded in this divine act of salvation is that God becomes the Christian's all in all. This seems to be the purport of the list of titles given to God at the close of this text.

The Christian Community and Its Witness to the Truth

Finally, the author of this letter presents two "evidences" for the truth of Christianity. The first is the Christian community. Diognetus, like many other pagans, had been amazed at the love Christians showed for one another. Here is how Lucian of Samosata (ca. 115–ca. 200), a pagan satirist, portrays the Christian church in his satire *The Passing of Peregrinus*, which deals with the career of a shyster by that name. For a while in his career Peregrinus pretended to be a Christian and became a teacher in a Christian community in Asia Minor. Finding himself in prison for his professed faith, Peregrinus was soon the center of attention from members of the church. "First thing every morning," Lucian wrote, "you would see a crowd of old women, widows, and orphans waiting outside the prison" bringing him "all sorts of food." In fact, Lucian went on to say, Christians "are always incredibly quick off the mark, when one of them gets into trouble like this—in fact they ignore their own interests completely." And why do they do this? Well, Lucian explained to his pagan audience, the Christians' "law-giver," by whom he means Christ, "has convinced them that once they stop believing in Greek gods, and start worshipping that crucified sage of theirs, and living according to his laws, they are all each other's brothers and sisters."[35] Coming from a pagan author not at all well disposed toward Christianity,

---

[34] *The Early Church* (Harmondsworth, UK: Penguin, 1967), 55.
[35] *The Passing of Peregrinus* 11–13, in *Lucian: Satirical Sketches*, trans. Paul Turner (Harmondsworth, UK: Penguin, 1961), 11.

this is a remarkable testimony to the way in which many early Christian communities were centers of love.

Pagan life was characterized by passions quite different. "Living in malice and envy, hateful and hating one another" (Titus 3:3, NKJV) is the way that Paul depicts the social fabric of the empire in the first century. No wonder, then, Christian communities stood out like brilliant lights in a dark firmament (Phil. 2:14–15). And no wonder, according to the first chapter of this treatise, Diognetus asked, "What is the warm fraternal affection they [i.e., believers] all feel for one another?"

The answer our unknown author gives is found in the final extant chapter of the treatise.

> God loved the race of men. It was for their sakes that he made the world; it was to them that he gave dominion over everything in it. On them he bestowed reason and understanding, and they alone received permission to lift their eyes to him. He formed them in his own image; he sent his only-begotten Son to them; he promised them the kingdom of heaven, and to those who have loved him he will surely give it. Once you have grasped these truths, think how your joy will overflow, and what love you will feel for him who loved you so.[36]

Christians love one another because God first loved them and showed that love through the sacrificial gift of his own beloved Son. Embracing the Son's death for one's sins by faith alone—earlier the author stated that God "has only revealed himself to faith, by which alone are we permitted to know God"[37]—leads to a desire to imitate God, the great lover of mankind. And it is in the mutual love of believers for one another and for their neighbors that evidence will be seen that "God lives in heaven" (10.7). Christian love is thus one key evidence for the truth of the Christian worldview.

Our author discerns a second evidence for the truth of Christianity in the way that believers were prepared to swim against the stream of their contemporaries' ethical values and even to die for their beliefs. Earlier in the treatise, the author stresses that Christians are not distinguished from their culture by virtue of their geographical location, language, or customs of dress, food, and other matters of daily life (5.1–2, 4). In other words, Christians did

---

[36] *Letter to Diognetus* 10.2–3, in Staniforth, *Early Christian Writings*, 148, altered.
[37] *Letter to Diognetus* 8.6, in Staniforth, *Early Christian Writings*, 147, altered.

not seek to escape from involvement in their society. Yet, their worldview did draw certain lines of demarcation between themselves and their surrounding culture. The fact that they were destined for heaven, "a world of holy love," to quote a later Christian author, Jonathan Edwards (1703–1758), meant that their lives in this world were ordered differently from that of their pagan neighbors. In essence, they lived in the world, in various communities scattered around the Mediterranean basin, but they did not live their lives in accord with this world's standards (5.5, 8–9). In particular, this paradoxical relationship to their society is well seen in their attitude toward child exposure and sexual expression.

Child Exposure and Sex

In common with the rest of Graeco-Roman society Christians married and bore children (5.6). Unlike their culture, however, they utterly refused to engage in the practice of child exposure: "They marry and beget children, though they do not expose their infants."[38] This practice of placing unwanted babies out in the streets or on the edge of town near the garbage dumps was all too common throughout the Graeco-Roman world. The wealthy did not want to share their worldly wealth among too many heirs; the poor had too many mouths to feed. A frank statement of this practice has been found recently in a letter written around the year 1 BC by a man who was away on a business trip. He instructed his pregnant wife in Alexandria, who was about to give birth, "When you give birth, if it is male leave it, if a female, cast it out."[39]

The New Testament nowhere explicitly condemns the practice of abortion, which is somewhat surprising in view of the fact that abortion was not at all uncommon in the Graeco-Roman world.[40] Whatever the reason for this explicit silence, early Christian authors outside of the New Testament consistently saw in the frequent recourse to abortion by women in the Graeco-Roman world a violation of the scriptural prohibition against murder. For instance, the second-century apologist Athenagoras (fl. 170s), a contemporary

---

[38] Letter to Diognetus 5.6, in Staniforth, Early Christian Writings, 145.

[39] Papyrus Oxyrhynchus 4.744.

[40] For the Graeco-Roman view of abortion, see Richard Harrow Fein, "Abortion and Exposure in Ancient Greece: Assessing the Status of the Fetus and 'Newborn' from Classical Sources," in Abortion and the Status of the Fetus, ed. William B. Bondeson et al. (Dordrecht: Reidel, 1983), 283–300; Michael J. Gorman, Abortion and the Early Church (Downers Grove, IL: InterVarsity, 1982), 13–32. For a discussion of the implicit evidence of the New Testament with regard to abortion, see Gorman, Abortion, 48. Gorman's book, currently out of print, remains the best book-length study of this issue.

of the author of the *Letter to Diognetus*, answered the pagan accusation that Christians practiced cannibalism thus:

> What sense does it make to think of us as murderers when we say that women who practice abortion are murderers and will render account to God for abortion? The same man cannot regard that which is in the womb as a living being and for that reason an object of God's concern and then murder it when it has come into the light.[41]

Substantially, this was to be the position with regard to abortion that the church would maintain throughout the Patristic era. It was part and parcel of a much larger attitude toward the physically weak and infirm. Whereas the pagan Graeco-Roman world was extremely callous with regard to the value of human life, early Christian communities as a whole sought to demonstrate the compassion of the Lord Jesus for the weak and defenseless.[42]

A second area where the Christian communities differed radically from their culture was in the area of sexual ethics: "Any Christian is free to share his neighbour's table, but never his marriage-bed."[43] Sexual immorality was rampant within the empire, but Christians were firm in their stand against it. As this author and other Christian apologists emphasized, charges of sexual immorality against the Christians were groundless.[44]

The Martyrs

Like many cultures, though, those of the Roman Empire responded to such nonconformity with fear and hatred, ostracism and persecution. This hatred and the Christian response to it is mentioned a number of times in the letter. For example, in chapter 5 of this treatise we read this about these early Christians:

> They show love to all men—and all men persecute them. They are misunderstood, and condemned; yet by suffering death they are quickened into life. They are poor, yet making many rich; lacking all things, yet having all

---

[41] *Plea on Behalf of the Christians* 35.6, in *Athenagoras: Legatio and De Resurrectione*, trans. William R. Schoedel (Oxford: Clarendon, 1972), 85. For a discussion of this text from Athenagoras, see Gorman, *Abortion*, 53–54. On the charge of cannibalism, see below, chapter 5.

[42] It is noteworthy that one of the major reasons for the successful expansion of the church throughout the Roman Empire was the practical expression of love that Christians showed for one another and for unbelievers. See Henry Chadwick, *The Early Church*, rev. ed. (London: Penguin, 1993), 56–58.

[43] *Letter to Diognetus* 5.7, in Staniforth, *Early Christian Writings*, 145.

[44] See, for example, Theophilus of Antioch, *To Autolycus* 3.4.

things in abundance. They are dishonoured, yet made glorious in their very dishonour; slandered, yet vindicated. They repay calumny with blessings, and abuse with courtesy. For the good they do, they suffer stripes as evildoers; and under the strokes they rejoice like men given new life. Jews assail them as heretics, and Greeks harass them with persecutions; and yet of all their ill-wishers there is not one who can produce good grounds for his hostility.[45]

As this passage lays bare, Christians were verbally abused by their fellow Greeks and Romans, despoiled, put on trial as evildoers, and condemned to death. Notice, though, how they reacted—with love: "They show love to all men."

As noted above, in the Roman Empire the mode of executing enemies of the state and criminals varied, for Roman punishment was tailored to the social status of the criminal rather than the crime. Thus, beheading was the major form of execution for citizens of the empire who committed a capital offense. Others would be exposed to a whole range of horrific means of execution, including burning and being mauled to death by ferocious beasts. Both of the latter are mentioned in this letter. In 10.8 we read of believers who "endure for righteousness' sake a transient flame."[46] And at the close of chapter 7 the author mentions death by wild beasts:

[Have you not seen Christians] flung to the wild beasts to make them deny their Lord, and yet remaining undefeated? Do you not see how the more of them suffer such punishments, the larger grows the number of the rest? These things do not look like the work of man; they are the power of God, and the evident tokens of his presence.[47]

The way in which the author views the martyrdoms of believers is noteworthy. They are, first of all, a means by which the church grows. As the North African theologian Tertullian once put it, "the blood of Christians is seed," that is, the seedbed of the church.[48] Second, the author of the *Letter to Diognetus* sees in the steadfastness of the martyrs nothing less than a

---

[45]*Letter to Diognetus* 5.11–17, in Staniforth, *Early Christian Writings*, 145.

[46]*Letter to Diognetus* 10.8, in Staniforth, *Early Christian Writings*, 149, altered.

[47]*Letter to Diognetus* 7.8, in Staniforth, *Early Christian Writings*, 146. At the beginning of this verse there is a gap in the manuscript, and the material enclosed in square brackets is supplied to make sense of what follows.

[48]*Apology* 50.13, in *Tertullian: Apologetical Works and Minucius Felix: Octavius*, trans. Emily Joseph Daly, Rudolph Arbesmann, and Edwin A. Quain (New York: Fathers of the Church, 1950), 125.

proof for the truth of the martyrs' testimony. We have already seen this in the witness of Ignatius of Antioch, and now we catch a glimpse of the same idea here. Apologetics in the ancient church took place not only by means of reasoning through the spoken word and such tracts as this letter, but also in the midst of horrific martyrdoms. Justin Martyr, so named for his own martyrdom, was brought to Christ by watching the way that believers died in the arena. "When I myself reveled in the teachings of Plato," he tells us, "and heard the Christians misrepresented and watched them stand fearless in the face of death and every other thing that was considered fearful, I realized the impossibility of their living in sinful pleasure."[49] Similarly, Tertullian spoke of the apologetic power of those who shed their blood for their love of Christ: "Whoever beholds such noble endurance will first, as though struck by some kind of uneasiness, be driven to enquire what is the matter in question, and, then, when he knows the truth, immediately follow the same way."[50]

Patristic Apologetics: Some Principles

What central aspects of Patristic apologetics do we find in this theological pearl? First, there is the recognition of the vital importance of prayer. The author mentions right at the beginning of his treatise that he is praying for Diognetus's conversion. He is very aware that unless Diognetus is given ears to hear the truth, all efforts to write this treatise for him will be in vain. Linked with this is the author's conviction that men and women are unable to reason their way to the truth without God's help. If God is to be found, he must reveal himself to the seeking heart. The author thus stresses the provision that God has made for finding him through the revelation of himself in his Son, Jesus Christ. Third, and understandably, the death of Christ for sinners also plays a prominent role in his witness to the true God. It is the death of the Son that frees men and women from shame and bondage, and thus enables them to genuinely participate in God's love, both as recipients and as agents of love to others. Then, too, he recognizes the importance of the Christian community as a vehicle of witness, in their love for one another, their life together, and even their dying for their faith.

To pick up on this final point of dying for one's faith: this treatise is a marvelous witness to the fact that the ancient church knew there are some

---

[49] *Second Apology* 12, in *Saint Justin Martyr*, trans. Thomas B. Falls (New York: Christian Heritage, 1948), 132.
[50] *To Scapula* 5, in Daly, Arbesmann, and Quain, *Tertullian: Apologetical Works*, 161.

things more important than life itself. In the words of Justin Martyr, "The lover of truth must choose, in every way possible, to do and say what is right, even when threatened with death, rather than save his own life."[51] J. G. O'Neill has noted the "overwhelming sense of the uniqueness of the Christian religion [that] dominates the . . . thought" of the author of this treatise. As proof, O'Neill points to the author's argument in chapters 5 and 6 that what the soul is to the body, Christians are to the world. The conception that this community of Christians had a vital role in the sustaining of the world might have sounded ludicrous to many of the writer's pagan contemporaries, but O'Neill is right to see in it the author's unshakeable confidence about Christian truth.[52] It was a conviction that was rooted in the New Testament and permeated the ancient church's witness to a sin-shaped culture.

---

[51] *First Apology* 2.1, in Falls, *Saint Justin Martyr*, 34.
[52] "Epistle to Diognetus," 104–6.

Chapter 4

INTERPRETING THE SCRIPTURES

The Exegesis of Origen

We have received not the spirit of the world, but the Spirit who is from God,
that we might understand the things freely given us by God. And we impart
this in words not taught by human wisdom but taught by the Spirit,
interpreting spiritual truths to those who are spiritual.

1 CORINTHIANS 2:12–13

Origen, nicknamed Adamantius, "Man of Steel,"[1] was born into a very wealthy Christian home around 185 in Egypt.[2] His father, Leonides, recognized Origen's giftedness when he was a young child and subsequently gave him a superb education in both Greek literature and

---

[1] Jerome, *On Illustrious Men* 54, in *Saint Jerome: On Illustrious Men*, trans. Thomas P. Halton (Washington, DC: The Catholic University of America Press, 1999), 77.
[2] Extremely helpful in the study of the life and thought of Origen are Henri Crouzel, *Origen*, trans. A. S. Worrall (San Francisco: Harper and Row, 1989); Joseph W. Trigg, *Origen* (London: Routledge, 1998); and John Anthony McGuckin, ed., *The Westminster Handbook to Origen* (Louisville, KY: Westminster John Knox, 2004). See also Rowan A. Greer's very helpful introduction to Origen's piety in *Origen: An Exhortation to Martyrdom, Prayer, First Principles: Book IV, Prologue to the Commentary on the Song of Songs, Homily XXVII on Numbers*, trans. Greer, The Classics of Western Spirituality (New York: Paulist, 1979), 1–37; hereafter this translation will be cited as Greer, *Origen*.

the Scriptures.[3] The latter involved memorization of most of the Greek Bible, which would serve Origen in good stead when he became the foremost biblical exegete of his day. Leonides, though, was beheaded during a persecution in Alexandria in 202.[4] Eusebius of Caesarea (ca. 260–338/339), sometimes described as the "father of church history" because of his invaluable work on the history of the church up to his day and a man devoted to the memory of Origen,[5] tells us that when Origen learned of the arrest and imprisonment of his father, he was determined to join him in prison. His mother tried to reason him out of his resolve, but to no avail. So she hid his clothes from him, and thus he was compelled to stay at home till after his father's death![6] Origen, though, never forgot that his father was a martyr.[7]

Since the property of condemned Christians was confiscated by the imperial treasury, Origen and his family were now destitute. It was only through the generosity of a rich Christian widow that Origen could still continue his studies. In 206 another bout of persecution forced all of the teachers in Alexandria into hiding. Origen took their place until he was denounced by neighbors and narrowly escaped arrest at his home. Despite the very evident danger, Origen continued to teach in various house churches in Alexandria. At least seven of his students died as martyrs during this particular persecution.[8]

After the cessation of this bout of violence against the church, and though Origen was but a young man, he was appointed the head of the catechetical school in Alexandria, where Clement of Alexandria (ca. 160–215) appears to have served before him. It was not long before Origen's fame as an interpreter of Scripture began to spread throughout Egypt and the eastern Mediterranean. He also became renowned for his holiness, though it needs to be noted that the story of his taking Matthew 19:12 literally and castrating himself is almost definitely apocryphal. It seems to have had its origins among those who later detested Origen's memory and were prepared to go to such lengths to discredit him.[9] In time, a certain Ambrose, who was converted out of

---

[3]Timothy D. Barnes, *Constantine and Eusebius* (Cambridge, MA: Harvard University Press, 1981), 82. I have drawn upon Barnes in structuring the brief sketch of Origen's life that follows.

[4]Jerome, *On Illustrious Men* 54, in Halton, *Saint Jerome: On Illustrious Men*, 77.

[5]On Eusebius, see Barnes, *Constantine and Eusebius*, passim, and Barnes, "Eusebius of Caesarea," *The Expository Times* 121 (2009): 1–14.

[6]*Church History* 6.2.

[7]*Homily on Ezekiel* 4.8.

[8]Barnes, *Constantine and Eusebius*, 83.

[9]It is mentioned by Eusebius in his *Church History* 6.8. See also Rowan Williams, "Origen," in *The First Theologians: An Introduction to Theology in the Early Church*, ed. G. R. Evans (Malden, MA: Blackwell, 2004), 133.

Valentinian Gnosticism by the teaching of Origen, became the Alexandrian theologian's patron and benefactor. He urged Origen to begin writing commentaries on the Scriptures, and to give his urging teeth he provided Origen with shorthand writers and copyists—a scriptorium with around twenty people or so working in it![10]—to take down the exegete's dictation and reproduce his books in multiple copies.[11]

Origen the Theologian

English historian Timothy D. Barnes has rightly noted that Origen was both a "speculative theologian of unparalleled boldness and imagination" and a profound interpreter of the Scriptures.[12] He authored *Against Celsus*, which was a reply to a pagan critic of Christianity and was the consummate work of this genre of apologetics in the Patristic era. Then, there were his doctrinal works, of which the chief is *On First Principles* (ca. 230), the first truly systematic theology, and lesser-known works like the *Dialogue with Heraclides*, found in a seventh-century Coptic codex in 1941 at Tura, some 12 kilometers south of Cairo during the clearing of rubbish from a limestone cave to make it a storage area for British munitions during the Second World War. The *Dialogue* is the lively transcript of an actual debate between the Arabian bishop Heraclides, who seems to have been suspected of modalism, and Origen, who has been asked to help Heraclides express his theology in an orthodox fashion. Modalism, or Sabellianism as it is sometimes called after Sabellius, a third-century errorist, all but eliminated any distinction between the persons of the Godhead. Origen is careful to stress that we must preserve the distinction of the Father and the Son in both thought and worship. At the same time he insists that we need to uphold the unity of the Father and the Son and so affirm the Son's deity.[13]

As for the Holy Spirit, Origen penned the first systematic consideration of the Spirit in his *On First Principles* 1.3, written in 229–230.[14] There he begins by establishing from Scripture the Spirit's personal existence and then goes on to tackle the issue of his deity. The baptismal formula of Matthew

---

[10]Hermann J. Vogt, "Origen of Alexandria (185–253)," in Charles Kannengiesser, *Handbook of Patristic Exegesis: The Bible in Ancient Christianity*, vol. 1 (Leiden: E. J. Brill, 2004), 539.
[11]Barnes, *Constantine and Eusebius*, 84.
[12]Ibid., 86.
[13]*Dialogue with Heraclides* 1–4.
[14]For what follows regarding Origen's views on the deity of the Spirit, I am drawing from my *The Spirit of God: The Exegesis of 1 and 2 Corinthians in the Pneumatomachian Controversy of the Fourth Century* (Leiden: E. J. Brill, 1994), 9–18.

28:19–20 points the way here for Origen, since it joins "the name of the Holy Spirit . . . to that of the unbegotten God the Father and his only-begotten Son."[15] These words reflect a clear conviction to exclude the Spirit from the created realm. In fact, at this point, Origen states that he has been unable to find any "passage in the holy scriptures which would warrant us in saying the Holy Spirit was a being made or created."[16]

In a portion of another work, however—namely, his commentary on the Gospel of John, written around the same time as *On First Principles*—Origen seems more hesitant to call the Spirit fully divine. Origen's starting point is the Johannine verse, "All things were made through him" (John 1:3). He writes:

> If then it is acknowledged as true that "all things were brought into being through him," we must enquire whether the Holy Spirit was brought into being through him. It seems to me that anyone who asserts that he was brought into being and who accepts that "all things were brought into being through him" will have to admit that the Holy Spirit was brought into being through the Word and that the Word is senior to him. And it follows that anyone who is reluctant to describe the Holy Spirit as brought into being through Christ must—if he accepts the statements of this gospel as true— say that he is unbegotten.
>
> There is a third possibility in addition either to allowing that the Holy Spirit was brought into being or to supposing that he is unbegotten. It would be possible for someone to claim that the Holy Spirit does not have any individual existence in distinction from the Father and the Son. But perhaps such a person would be ready to agree that, if one regards the Son as distinct from the Father, it will be a matter of the Spirit being identical with the Father, since there seems to be a clear distinction between the Spirit and the Son in the text: "Whoever speaks a word against the son of man, it will be forgiven him; but whoever blasphemes against the Holy Spirit will have no forgiveness in this age or in the age to come" [Matt. 12:32].[17]

As to the origin of the Spirit, Origen envisages three possibilities: (1) the Spirit is a creature of the Son; (2) the Spirit is unbegotten like the Father; (3) the Spirit has no being of his own, but is identical with the Father. Origen

---

[15] *On First Principles* 1.2, in *Origen: On First Principles*, trans. G. W. Butterworth (1966; repr., Gloucester, MA: Peter Smith, 1973), 30; hereafter this translation will be cited as Butterworth, *Origen: On First Principles*.

[16] *On First Principles* 1.3, in Butterworth, *Origen: On First Principles*, 31.

[17] *Commentary on John* 2.10, in *Documents in Early Christian Thought*, trans. Maurice Wiles and Mark Santer (Cambridge: Cambridge University Press, 1975), 78.

rejects the last two possibilities. The one, that the Spirit is unbegotten, is a violation of Origen's theological premise that God the Father alone is unbegotten. The other, that the Spirit is identical with the Father, was the position of late second-century and third-century modalism.[18] For advocates of this heresy, the Father, the Son, and the Spirit are simply adjectival descriptions of temporary modes of being that the one God adopts in the implementation of the various stages of divine activity: creation, salvation, and sanctification. Numerous texts bear witness to Origen's vigorous opposition to this conception of God,[19] and his rejection of the third possibility as to the origin of the Spirit is thus a foregone conclusion.

Consequently, Origen endorses the first possibility as the best explanation for the origin of the Spirit. He writes:

> The view which asks our approval as the most religious and truthful one is the following: that of all things brought into being through the Word the Holy Spirit is the most honourable and he is first in rank of all the things brought into being by the Father through Christ. And perhaps this is the reason why the Spirit is not called a son of God as well. The only-begotten alone is a son by nature from the very beginning; whereas the Holy Spirit seems to require the Son as an intermediary in respect of his distinct existence—not merely enabling him to exist but enabling him to exist as wise, rational, just and with all the other characteristics he must be thought of as having by participation in the attributes of Christ, of which we have spoken earlier.[20]

This passage appears to place the Holy Spirit in the realm of those creatures made by the Father through the mediation of the Son. Yet, in order to understand this text correctly it is important to recall that prior to the Council of Nicaea in 325, no distinction was made between "uncreated" (*agenētos*)

---

[18]On modalism, see Jaroslav Pelikan, *The Christian Tradition: A History of the Development of Doctrine,* vol. 1, *The Emergence of the Catholic Tradition (100–600)* (Chicago: University of Chicago Press, 1971), 176–82.

[19]For example, see *Commentary on Romans* 8.5; *Against Celsus* 8.12. For a discussion of Origen's opposition to modalism, see Adolf von Harnack, *Handbuch der Dogmengeschichte,* 3rd. ed. (Freiburg: Akademische Verlagsbuchhandlung von J. C. B. Mohr [Paul Siebeck], 1894), 1:720–22; Jean Daniélou, *Gospel Message and Hellenistic Culture,* trans. and ed. J. A. Baker (London: Darton, Longman & Todd; Philadelphia: Westminster Press, 1973), 376–77; Norbert Brox, "Spiritualität und Orthodoxie: Zum Konflikt des Origenes mit der Geschichte des Dogmas," in *Pietas: Festschrift für Bernhard Kotting,* ed. Ernst Dassman and K. S. Drunk, Jahrbuch für Antike und Christentum 8 (Münster: Aschendorffsche Verlagsbuchhandlung, 1980), 140–54, passim.

[20]*Commentary on John* 2.10, in Wiles and Santer, *Documents,* 78.

and "unbegotten" (*agennētos*), or between "created" (*genētos*) and "begotten" (*gennētos*).[21] Since Origen regards only the Father as *agenētos*/*agennētos*, the Spirit (and the Son) have to be *genēton*/*gennēton*, a term that was used also to describe the created realm in contrast to God. Nevertheless, other texts definitely indicate that Origen understands the Spirit (and the Son) to be radically different from the rest of the created realm since he (along with the Son) possesses all the qualities of divine life substantially, whereas the creatures possess them only accidentally.[22] Furthermore, Origen regards the substantial possession of these qualities by the Spirit as eternal.[23] Accordingly, the Spirit's "creation" by the Father through the Son must be considered an eternal one. As Origen says in his *Commentary on Romans*, "The Spirit himself is in the law and in the gospel; he is ever with the Father and the Son; like the Father and the Son he always is, and was, and will be."[24]

The Spirit is thus distinct from the created realm and definitely a member of the Godhead despite the fact that Origen's imprecise terminology in his commentary on John gives the opposite impression. Nevertheless, the central concern of Origen in *Commentary on John* 2.10 is not the affirmation of the Spirit's divinity, but the demonstration of the reality of the Spirit's distinct existence. The "creation" of the Spirit by the Father through the mediation of the Son establishes this fact. This argument for the Holy Spirit's distinct existence will also be the basis upon which Basil of Caesarea, and his fellow Cappadocians—Gregory of Nazianzus and Gregory of Nyssa—develop the coequality of the Spirit with the Father and the Son in the following century.[25]

---

[21]G. L. Prestige, *God in Patristic Thought* (London: William Heinemann, 1936), 134–38; *Origène: Traité des Principes*, trans. Henri Crouzel and Manlio Simonetti, Sources Chrétiennes 252 (Paris: Les Éditions du Cerf), 1:37–43.

[22]For example, see *On First Principles* 1.6.2, where Origen states that in created rational beings "goodness does not reside substantially, as it does in God and his Christ and in the Holy Spirit. For only in the Trinity, which is the source of all things, does goodness reside substantially. All others possess it accidentally" (Butterworth, *Origen: On First Principles*, 53, revised). For other texts, see Jacques Dupuis, '*L'Esprit de l'homme*': *Étude sur l'anthropologie réligieuse d'Origène*, Museum Lessianum, Section Théologique 62 (Paris: Desclée de Brouwer, 1967), 92n12; D. L. Balas, "The Idea of Participation in the Structure of Origen's Thought: Christian Transposition of a Theme of the Platonic Tradition," in *Origeniana*, ed. Henri Crouzel et al., Quaderni di Vetera Christianorum 12 (Bari: Università di Bari, Istituto di Letteratura Cristiana Antica, 1975), 260n7.

[23]See, for example, *On First Principles* 4.4.1.

[24]*Commentary on Romans* 6.7, in *The Early Christian Fathers*, trans. Henry Bettenson (London: Oxford University Press, 1969), 227.

[25]See below, chapter 6.

But Origen also lays the groundwork for the thinking of those who would deny the deity of the Spirit (and the Son) in the following century. Since Origen holds God to be, by definition, One and uncompounded, the existence of Three within the Godhead is deeply problematic for him. He solves this dilemma by declaring that only God the Father is God in the proper sense of the term, and he thus places the Son and the Spirit on a level subordinate to the Father. His *Commentary on John* 13.25 contains a clear affirmation of this subordination. It states:

> We are convinced by the Savior's statement "the Father who sent me is greater than I" [John 14:28]. For this reason he did not bear to accept the appellation "good" in its proper sense of "true and perfect," when it was bestowed on him, but he offered it up gratefully to the Father with censure for the one who exceedingly praises the Son. [Thus] we say that the Savior, and the Holy Spirit, transcend all the creatures, not by degree but by a transcendence beyond measure. But he [the Son, like the Holy Spirit] is transcended by the Father as much as, or even more than, he and the Holy Spirit transcend the other creatures, even the highest.[26]

This text emphasizes Origen's belief that while the Son and the Spirit belong within the divine sphere, they are definitely inferior to the Father. While some scholars hold that this inferiority may be only economic and not ontological, the impression is given that the Son and the Spirit are both "middle beings," whereas the Father alone is God in the proper sense of the term.[27] Here then is the soil out of which Arianism sprang in the following century.[28]

It is passages like the one above regarding the "subordination" of the Son and the Spirit, as well as Origen's speculations about the possible salvation of the Devil and that created souls have an eternal existence before embodiment,[29] that led some at the close of the Patristic era to write him off as having gone

---

[26] *Commentary on John* 13.25 (my translation). Origen's *Commentary on Matthew* 15.10 should be compared with this passage from his commentary on John. In Matthew, Origen modifies the position taken in the passage cited above: the transcendence of the Son with regard to the created realm is greater than the transcendence of God the Father with regard to the Son. For a discussion of these two passages, see Daniélou, *Gospel Message*, 383–84.

[27] See T. E. Pollard, *Johannine Christology and the Early Church* (Cambridge: Cambridge University Press, 1970), 91–105.

[28] For Arianism, see chapter 6.

[29] On the preexistence of human souls, see Fred Norris, "Origen," in Philip F. Esler, ed., *The Early Christian World* (London: Routledge, 2000), 2:1019. There is evidence that Origen came to reject the idea of the salvation of the Devil as totally absurd (ibid., 2:1020).

beyond the bounds of Christian orthodoxy.[30] In this regard, it needs to be remembered that a paragon of orthodoxy like Basil of Caesarea thought Origen's works worth reading closely for theological and spiritual gems—he and his close friend Gregory of Nazianzus edited an anthology of such passages, the *Philocalia* (358–359)—even though he knew that Origen's ideas about the Spirit were not always sound.[31] The words of Robert Murray M'Cheyne (1813–1843) after hearing of the death of Edward Irving (1792–1834)—the preaching wonder of the 1820s, though a man who argued that the Son of God assumed sinful humanity—seem apropos of Origen: he was "a holy man in spite of all his delusions and errors."[32] And we need to take most seriously Origen's expressed desire when he says, "I want to be a man of the church, not the founder of heresy. I want to be named with Christ's name and bear that name, which is blessed on earth. I long to both be and be called a Christian as much in deed as in thought."[33]

Origen's Pioneer Biblical Studies

Essentially, though, Origen needs to be remembered as a Bible commentator who was primarily concerned with a christological exegesis of the Scriptures. Before Origen, there were few Christians who had tried to compose commentaries on books of either the Old Testament or the New.[34] The fourth-century Latin author and commentator Jerome notes on one occasion that he happened to see a commentary on Proverbs purportedly by Theophilus, the bishop of Antioch and apologist. Jerome, however, had his doubts that it was really the work of the second-century author. Origen's predecessor at the school in Alexandria, Clement, had written a work entitled *Hypotyposes*, which is said to have explained both the Old and New Testaments, but the few extant fragments of it deal only with the New. The one Christian commentator prior to Origen—and he was really an older contemporary of Origen—who wrote commentaries on parts of the Bible that have come down to us was Hippolytus (d. ca. 236), an elder at Rome in the early third

---

[30]See the brief discussions in Greer's introduction to his *Origen*, 28–31, and Norris, "Origen," 2:1006–8.

[31]*On the Holy Spirit* 29.73. On Origen's influence on Basil and the Cappadocians, see the brief remarks of Greer, "Introduction," in his *Origen*, 29.

[32]Andrew A. Bonar, *The Life of Robert Murray M'Cheyne* (Edinburgh: Banner of Truth, 1960), 35.

[33]*Homily on Luke* 16.6 (my translation).

[34]For many of the details in this section on Origen's biblical studies, I am indebted to Joseph T. Lienhard, "Origen and the Crisis of the Old Testament in the Early Church," *Pro Ecclesia* 9, no. 3 (2000): 360.

century whom Origen had heard preach on one occasion when he traveled to Rome in 212.[35] From Hippolytus we have the first extant Christian
commentary on any book of the Old Testament, namely, the prophecy of
Daniel. There is also a part of Hippolytus's commentary on the Song of
Songs that survives. We also know that Hippolytus penned commentaries
on other sections of the Old Testament, including the Psalms, Genesis, and
the prophets Isaiah, Ezekiel, and Zechariah, but all of these various commentaries are lost.

Origen appears to have been a man of prodigious energy when it came
to biblical studies. He prepared the enormous Hexapla, a set of books in
which the Hebrew Old Testament, its Greek transliteration, and various
Greek translations of the Old Testament known to Origen were written out
in parallel columns. The entirety probably ran to at least six thousand pages.
Sadly it was never recopied in its entirety and probably was destroyed by the
Muslim conquest of Palestine in the seventh century. Only fragments remain
and a more or less complete Syriac version.

Then, there were Origen's commentaries on both the Old and New
Testaments.[36] For example, when it came to commentaries on the Old Testament, he wrote thirteen books on Genesis, thirty-six on Isaiah, twenty-five
on Ezekiel, twenty-five on the Minor Prophets, thirty-five on the Psalms,
three on Proverbs, ten on the Song of Songs, and five on Lamentations.
In all, there were close to three hundred books of commentary, though
the vast majority of these have been lost. However, expository sermons
on large parts of the Old Testament—the Pentateuch, Joshua and Judges,
1 Kings, Isaiah, Jeremiah, Ezekiel, the Psalms, Job, Proverbs, Ecclesiastes,
and the Song of Songs—have survived. As for the New Testament, there
are extant commentaries on Matthew and John. Origen was the first to
write a commentary on all of the Pauline Epistles, although except for his
commentary on Romans (in a Latin translation and with a few portions
in Greek), only fragments of these commentaries have survived. There are
also extant homilies on the Gospels. Again, though, a vast amount of these
biblical homilies have not come down to us. As Patristic historian Fred
Norris notes of this loss, "The decision not to copy them [that is, these

---

[35] John McGuckin, "A Christian Philosophy: Origen," in Jonathan Hill, *The New Lion Handbook: The History of Christianity* (Oxford: Lion Hudson, 2007), 67.

[36] For the details in this paragraph, I am reliant on Lienhard, "Origen and the Crisis of the Old Testament," 362–63, and Norris, "Origen," 2:1010–11, though Lienhard and Norris sometimes differ in terms of some of the numbers.

commentaries and homilies], or to suppress them . . . leaves us without the many insights into Christian spirituality and mysticism which so richly enhanced much of Origen's corpus."[37]

There is little doubt that Origen pioneered the Christian study of the Old Testament. In fact, Joseph T. Lienhard has made a strong case that when, in the second and third centuries, the church was involved in a battle royal with the heresy of Gnosticism, which generally rejected the entire Old Testament as divine revelation, this battle was decisively concluded only with Origen's massive exegetical program that highlighted the writings of the old covenant and showed beyond a shadow of doubt that the Old Testament had to be included in the Christian Bible.[38]

Relocating to Caesarea and Being a Confessor

In 230, Origen left Alexandria for Caesarea in Palestine owing to a dispute with his bishop, Demetrius. On a previous visit to Caesarea, Origen had been ordained, an ordination that Demetrius regarded as invalid, even though bishops in Palestine, Phoenicia, Arabia, and Greece stood by Origen.[39] As a result, Origen left Alexandria for good. In Caesarea, with the ongoing help of Ambrose, he set up a form of a Christian seminary based on communal living.[40] It is noteworthy that the more speculative works of Origen—including *On First Principles*—were written in Alexandria, while the majority of his homilies—those on the Heptateuch, Jeremiah, Ezekiel, Song of Songs, Luke—and the biblical commentaries—the latter books of his commentary on John and the commentaries on Genesis, Psalms, the Song of Songs, Romans, and Matthew—date from the time in Caesarea.[41]

In the course of his *Commentary on Matthew*, which Origen wrote in 248–249, he made a striking comment on Matthew 24:9 ("Then they will deliver you up to tribulation and put you to death, and you will be hated by all nations for my name's sake"). Origen reckoned that there had not yet been an empire-wide persecution of Christians, but that, when such a persecution did transpire, then surely the words of verse 10, "and then many will fall away," would also take place. Within a year or so, Origen's prediction was

---

[37]Norris, "Origen," 2:1010.

[38]Lienhard, "Origen and the Crisis of the Old Testament," 355–66.

[39]Edgar J. Goodspeed, *A History of Early Christian Literature*, rev. ed., ed. Robert M. Grant (Chicago: University of Chicago Press, 1966), 135.

[40]Barnes, *Constantine and Eusebius*, 84–85.

[41]Gerard E. Caspary, *Politics and Exegesis: Origen and the Two Swords* (Berkeley: University of California Press, 1979), 7.

fulfilled. Those Christians who were younger than Origen, then in his mid-sixties, had never really experienced persecution. In 249, however, a Roman general from Illyria named Trajan Decius (r. 249–251) became emperor and launched a vicious persecution of the church. An imperial order for all citizens to sacrifice to the Roman gods was issued, and the Decian persecution, for so it has come to be called, was unleashed against the church. There were many who denied their faith or tried to buy certificates that indicated that they had sacrificed. Origen himself was arrested and imprisoned. The judge trying his case was not interested in putting him to death and thereby creating a famous martyr. Rather, he wanted to so torture Origen that the exegete would break and recant. But Origen did not succumb. Finally, after his body had been broken on the rack and the persecution had come to an end with Decius's death, he was set free. He subsequently died as a result of the torture he had experienced. Technically he was not a martyr, only a confessor—namely, one who was tried for his faith and who emerged alive. Some have reckoned that if he had died as a martyr, he might be remembered quite differently.[42] Nonetheless, Origen had undergone one of the greatest challenges a Christian of his day could face—and he had emerged victorious. His devotion to Christ, to his Word, and to his people was real—and Origen was willing to die for that devotion.

Interpreting the Scriptures

In light of the hostile view of Christianity by Graeco-Roman culture, it is noteworthy that Origen found it quite important to engage his culture. In fact, in doing so Origen showed that he was without a shadow of a doubt the greatest thinker of his day, pagan or Christian, one who was always writing to convince others of "the importance of Christian life and why a person should become a Christian."[43] His great work *Against Celsus* was a reasoned answer to the attacks of the pagan philosopher Celsus (fl. 160–180), who criticized the exclusive claims of Christianity as well as the doctrine of the incarnation in his *True Discourse* (ca. 170).[44] Many of Origen's theological works, particu-

---

[42]Trigg, *Origen*, 61.

[43]John Clark Smith, *The Ancient Wisdom of Origen* (Cranbury, NJ: Associated University Presses, 1992), 15.

[44]For an overview of Origen's *Against Celsus*, see Henry Chadwick's introduction to *Origen: Contra Celsum*, trans. Chadwick (Cambridge: Cambridge University Press, 1953), ix–xl (hereafter, Chadwick, *Origen: Contra Celsum*); Michael Frede, "Origen's Treatise *Against Celsus*," in Mark Edwards, Martin Goodman, and Simon Price, with Christopher Rowland, *Apologetics in the Roman Empire: Pagans, Jews, and Christians* (Oxford: Oxford University Press, 1999), 133–55.

larly *On First Principles*, also need to be seen as apologetic attempts to speak to the educated Greco-Roman culture around him, which was made up of a menagerie of pagan philosophies, mystery cults, Gnostic groups, and oriental religions. These two books, *Against Celsus* and *On First Principles*, clearly reveal that Origen's theological enterprise was not defined by the culture, but rather it was fundamentally shaped by mission to the culture. In many ways Origen succeeded in expounding Christianity in terms meaningful to the surrounding Graeco-Roman world.[45]

Central to Origen's engagement with Graeco-Roman culture was the Bible.[46] Although the Scriptures were often regarded as "barbaric" writings by educated Greeks and Romans, they played a vital role in the evangelization of the Roman Empire. Both Tatian (fl. 170s) and Theophilus of Antioch, for instance, directly attributed their conversions to reading the Scriptures.[47] Origen was firmly convinced that the Bible could effect such conversions because these "sacred books are not the works of men, but . . . they were composed and have come down to us as a result of the inspiration of the Holy Spirit by the will of the Father of the universe through Jesus Christ."[48] The emphasis here is on the activity of the Spirit: it is the Spirit who has "composed" or "supervised" the formation of the Scriptures.[49] Again, Origen can maintain, "Not only did the Spirit supervise the writings which were previous to the coming of Christ, but because he is the same Spirit and proceeds from the one God he has dealt in like manner with the gospels and the writings of the apostles."[50] Here, in the midst of affirming the divine authorship of the Scriptures, he also reaffirms a key hermeneutical principle found, for example, in his older contemporary Irenaeus of Lyons—namely, the unity of the Tes-

---

[45]Greer, "Introduction," in his *Origen*, 33.

[46]For two very helpful overviews of the various aspects of the ancient church's interpretation of the Bible, see James L. Kugel and Rowan A. Greer, *Early Biblical Interpretation* (Philadelphia: Westminster Press, 1986); and John J. O'Keefe and R. R. Reno, *Sanctified Vision: An Introduction to Early Christian Interpretation of the Bible* (Baltimore: John Hopkins University Press, 2005).

[47]See Tatian, *Address to the Greeks* 28–29; Theophilus of Antioch, *To Autolycus* 1.14. Michael Green notes: "From the Acts of the Apostles down to . . . Origen we find the same story repeated time and again. Discussion with Christians, arguments with them, annoyance at them, leads the enquirer to read these 'barbaric writings' [i.e., the Scriptures] for himself. And once men began to read, the Scriptures exercised their own fascination and power." *Evangelism in the Early Church* (Grand Rapids: Eerdmans, 1970), 234.

[48]*On First Principles* 4.2.2, in Butterworth, *Origen: On First Principles*, 272. See also *On First Principles* 4.2.7; 4.3.14.

[49]Michael W. Holmes, "Origen and the Inerrancy of Scripture," *Journal of the Evangelical Theological Society* 24 (1981): 221.

[50]*On First Principles* 4.2.9, in Butterworth, *Origen: On First Principles*, 287.

taments as being the work of one and the same Holy Spirit. As Origen told Celsus: "The gospel does not lay down laws in contradiction to the God of the law. . . . Nor did the Father forget when he sent Jesus the commands which he had given to Moses."[51]

Moreover, this work of the Spirit extends to every letter of Scripture: "The wisdom of God has penetrated to all the Scriptures inspired by God, even down to the smallest letter."[52] The result is that the entirety of the Scriptures can be called "the words of God."[53] For Origen, then, the true author of both the Old and New Testaments is the Holy Spirit.[54] A. Zöllig put it rightly when he stated, "[For Origen,] Holy Scripture has a divine nature, and this not simply because it contains divine ideas, nor because the breath of the divine Spirit breathes in its lines . . . but because it has God for its author."[55] In fact, the twentieth-century theologian Hans Urs von Balthasar has gone so far as to state that Origen "sacramentalized Scripture, stating that God's Spirit dwells in it with the same real presence as it does in the Church."[56]

All of this is vital for understanding Origen's exegesis. In the words of Origen scholar Ronald Heine, "We will not understand the way Origen reads the Bible if we miss this basic point, that it is always the Holy Spirit who speaks in the text of the Bible."[57] Every letter of Scripture is consequently of value, which explains why Origen devoted much time and energy to establishing the correct text of the Scriptures.

The value of the text, though, does not reside solely in the letter itself. Often it can be found only by going beyond the letter to the true meaning that the Spirit intends. If the exegete remains on the level of the letter of Scripture, he will be forced to acknowledge numerous illogical and impossible things as well as things that take away from God's divine majesty. The exegete must therefore go beyond or beneath the letter of Scripture to discover the spiritual meaning placed in hiding there by the Holy Spirit. Scripture is thus an encoded text.

---

[51] *Against Celsus* 7.25, in Chadwick, *Origen: Contra Celsum*, 415.

[52] *Philocalia* 2.4 (my translation).

[53] *On First Principles* 4.1.7, in Butterworth, *Origen: On First Principles*, 265.

[54] In *Against Celsus* 4.71, Origen can state alternatively, "The Logos of God seems to have arranged the Scriptures" (Chadwick, *Origen: Contra Celsum*, 240).

[55] Cited by Dan G. McCartney, "Literal and Allegorical Interpretation in Origen's *Contra Celsum*," *Westminster Theological Journal* 48 (1986): 287.

[56] Preface to Greer, *Origen*, xiii.

[57] "Reading the Bible with Origen," in *The Bible in Greek Christian Antiquity*, ed. Paul M. Blowers (Notre Dame, IN: University of Notre Dame Press, 1997), 132.

Origen's resort to allegorization—whereby, in the words of James L. Kugel, "biblical persons and incidents become representative of abstract virtues or doctrines or incidents in the life of the soul"[58]—was an embrace of what was a favored literary device in both Graeco-Roman academe and the world of Hellenistic Judaism. As early as the second century BC, Hellenistic Jewish writers, especially those based in Alexandria, were using allegorization to explain the Old Testament. They had derived it from their pagan Greek counterparts in the latter's reading of Homer. Greek allegorization of Homer was already widespread by the fifth century BC. According to Origen it originated with a certain Pherycedes of Syros (fl. ca. 600 BC).[59] So it was that in reading the Pentateuch, Hellenistic Jewish readers invariably encountered what were seemingly petty details—names of unfamiliar persons or places, or laws that seemed quite mundane. How might they best understand such things? Under the influence of Greek allegory, they sought a deeper meaning not immediately evident to a surface reading of the text.[60] It is vital to realize that this interest in allegorization led to the view that a historical text has transhistorical value only if it is capable of being allegorized. A text that is merely historical cannot be divine in its teachings.[61] Thus, the pagan critic Celsus charged that the Bible cannot be a divine book since it cannot be allegorized.[62]

Origen will also widely practice this method of exegesis.[63] However, he never uses allegory to the exclusion of other methods. He can use the familiar early Christian argument from prophecy, namely, that various Old Testament texts have a prophetic fulfillment in Christ, a method of interpretation found extensively, for example, in Justin Martyr's *Dialogue with Trypho*.[64] And Origen refuses to write off "merely" historical texts since those "passages which are historically true are far more numerous than those which are composed with purely spiritual meanings."[65]

Thus, Origen can frequently surprise the reader. Where one might expect him to drift off into allegory, he remains firmly wedded to the text. Consider

---

[58]Kugel and Greer, *Early Biblical Interpretation*, 81.

[59]*Against Celsus* 6.42. See McCartney, "Literal and Allegorical Interpretation," 282–83.

[60]Kugel and Greer, *Early Biblical Interpretation*, 81–82.

[61]McCartney, "Literal and Allegorical Interpretation," 283.

[62]Origen, *Against Celsus* 1.17–18. See also McCartney, "Literal and Allegorical Interpretation," 283.

[63]On Origen's allegorization, see the helpful overview by Thomas P. Scheck, "General Introduction," in *Origen: Homilies 1–14 on Ezekiel*, trans. Scheck, Ancient Christian Writers 62 (New York: Newman, 2010), 3–7.

[64]Kugel and Greer, *Early Biblical Interpretation*, 179.

[65]*On First Principles* 4.3.4, in Butterworth, *Origen: On First Principles*, 295.

his interpretation of Jephthah's vow (Judg. 11:29–40), which is found not in
his homily on the passage in Judges, but in some comments he made on John
1:29.[66] Although nine of Origen's homilies on Judges survive, these deal with
only Judges 1–7 and not Judges 11. Origen has just stated that the words
of John the Baptist in John 1:29 refer specifically to the humanity of Christ.
He then comments:

> This slain lamb has indeed become, according to certain ineffable reasons, a
> purification for the whole world on behalf of which, following the Father's
> loving plan, he even accepted immolation, redeeming us by his blood from
> him who had come into possession of us, [that is, Satan,] when we had
> been sold as slaves because of our sins. And the one leading this lamb to
> the sacrifice was God in man, the great high priest, who makes this clear
> with the words: "No one takes my life away from me, but I lay it down of
> my own accord. I have power to lay it down, and I have power to pick it up
> again" [John 10:18].[67]

Immediately after this, Origen links the deaths of various believers in the
Old Testament and "the shedding of the blood of the noble martyrs" to the
death of Christ.[68] The Old Testament sacrifices were "a symbol" of the death
of Christ, and in a similar way, the deaths of the martyrs bespeak the death of
Christ. One such similarity between the deaths of the martyrs and the death
of Christ is that the martyrs' deaths benefit the church, though obviously not
in any way equal to the Lord's consummate sacrifice. To understand more
clearly how their deaths can benefit others, Origen suggests meditating upon
the death of Jephthah's daughter.

Origen notes first of all that this story gives to God the appearance of
"great cruelty." Similarly, it might seem cruel for God to require martyrdom.[69]

---

[66]*Commentary on John* 6.35–36. This follows the numbering in the translation by Allan Menzies, *Epistle
to Gregory and Origen's Commentary on the Gospel of John*, The Ante-Nicene Fathers 10 (repr., Edinburgh:
T&T Clark; Grand Rapids: Eerdmans, 1986). On Origen's interpretation of Jephthah's daughter, I
have benefited from the comments of Robert J. Daly, "Sacrificial Soteriology: Origen's Commentary on
John 1,29," in *Origeniana Secunda*, ed. Henri Crouzel and Antonio Quacquarelli, Quaderni di "Vetera
Christianorum" 15 (Rome: Edizioni dell' Ateneo, 1980), 151–63; John L. Thompson, *Writing the
Wrongs: Women of the Old Testament among Biblical Commentators from Philo through the Reformation*
(Oxford: Oxford University Press, 2001), 113–14; Thompson, "Scripture, Tradition, and the Forma-
tion of Christian Culture: The Theological and Pastoral Function of the History of Interpretation," *Ex
Auditu* 19 (2003): 30–31.
[67]*Commentary on John* 6.53, in Daly, "Sacrificial Soteriology," in *Origeniana Secunda*, ed. Crouzel and
Quacquarelli, 156.
[68]Daly, "Sacrificial Soteriology," in *Origeniana Secunda*, ed. Crouzel and Quacquarelli, 156.
[69]Thompson, "Scripture, Tradition, and the Formation of Christian Culture," 30.

His response to this potential charge in both cases is threefold. Origen reminds his readers of the basic inability that humans have to understand the ways of God, in relation to which he quotes *Wisdom of Solomon* 17:1, "Great are your judgments and difficult to explain, because of which unschooled souls have erred." Origen seems to be saying that martyrdom might appear to be a waste, like the death of Jephthah's daughter, but the church must believe by faith that God uses it for good.[70] Origen then observes that even some pagans, to curb a plague or famine, have been known to offer themselves in sacrifice to their gods/goddesses. He thus asserts that Christians must believe that the deaths of the holy martyrs can indeed aid in breaking the bonds of demonic powers. What is noteworthy in this interpretation of the death of Jephthah's daughter is that Origen refuses to employ allegory to escape the difficulties of the text.

By and large, unlike pagan allegorizers, who saw no value in the literal text, Origen discerns three values in the literal text.[71] First, the Bible does indeed contain true and important history; to discard that would eviscerate Christianity. This is completely different from pagan allegorization and also quite different from that of the Alexandrian Jewish interpreter Philo (ca. 20 BC–ca. AD 50), who has no real sense of history. Thus, for example, Origen will defend the historicity of the events of Christ's life.[72] Or consider the trip that Origen took across Palestine to discover whether or not there was indeed a "Bethany beyond the Jordan," as John puts it (John 1:28).[73] Then, second, Origen was ever conscious that the church contained "simple" believers who are edified by the literal meaning of the text. Finally, the literal meaning does have a clear apologetic value. It is noteworthy that Origen is restrained in his use of allegory in *Against Celsus*, for instance.

All of this is very instructive for understanding Origen's use of allegory. In his opinion, one should not resort too easily to this method of interpretation. As Henry Chadwick notes, Origen excluded the literal sense only in rare cases.[74] And in the words of Gerald Bostock, "Origen was concerned to defend the historical foundations of Scripture on which he built his treasure

---

[70]Ibid.

[71]For these three values, see McCartney, "Literal and Allegorical Interpretation," 287–89.

[72]See *On First Principles* 4.3.4.

[73]*Commentary on John* 6.24. This follows the numbering in the translation by Menzies, *Epistle to Gregory and Origen's Commentary on the Gospel of John*.

[74]*The Church in Ancient Society: From Galilee to Gregory the Great* (Oxford: Oxford University Press, 2001), 137.

house of allegorical wisdom."[75] Origen thus explicitly condemned those who dispensed entirely with the historical element of Scripture. As Chadwick notes, Origen had before him Valentinian Gnosticism, which allegorized all too freely and in so doing committed the error of "dissolving history into timeless myth."[76]

And yet, while Origen clearly does not wish to discard history as worthless—such was the way of Gnostic exegesis—his exegetical methodology does not involve a robust adherence to the significance of history. In the words of R. P. C. Hanson: Origen "defends the historicity of most of the events recorded in the Bible. . . . But he perilously reduces the significance of history. . . . In his view history, if it is to have any significance at all, can be no more than an acted parable, a charade for showing forth eternal truths about God."[77] There is certainly some truth to this critique. For instance, Origen can assert that the chief value of a miracle is not that it actually happened, but the truth that is hidden within it.[78]

Three Principles of Interpretation

As one delves into Origen's exegesis, three further principles of interpretation emerge. First, the Scriptures must have a present meaning or application. Origen often cites 1 Corinthians 10:6 and 11 to emphasize the existential meaning of the Word of God. Commenting, for example, on the reference to mud and bricks in Exodus 1:14, he states: "These words were not written to teach us about history, nor must we think that the divine books narrate the acts of the Egyptians. But what has been written has been written for our instruction and admonition."[79] One sentence from his *Homilies on Genesis* sums up his approach in this regard. Commenting on Genesis 18:8, "[Abraham] stood . . . under the tree," Origen says, "What does it help me who have come to hear what the Holy Spirit teaches the human race, if I hear that 'Abraham was standing under a tree'?"[80]

---

[75]"Allegory and the Interpretation of the Bible in Origen," *Journal of Literature and Theology* 1, no. 1 (March 1987): 49.

[76]*Early Christian Thought and the Classical Tradition* (London: Oxford University Press, 1966), 11. Origen was therefore clear that allegorization was no guarantee of orthodoxy. See Vogt, "Origen of Alexandria," 537.

[77]R. P. C. Hanson, *Allegory and Event: A Study of the Sources and Significance of Origen's Interpretation of Scripture* (1959; repr., Louisville, KY: Westminster John Knox, 2002), 364.

[78]*Against Celsus* 2.48.

[79]*Homily on Exodus* 1.5 (my translation). For further uses of 1 Corinthians 10 in this regard, see also Mark Sheridan, "Scripture," in *Westminster Handbook to Origen*, ed. McGuckin, 199.

[80]Cited by Lienhard, "Origen and the Crisis of the Old Testament," 364.

Second, Origen sought to interpret the Scriptures in accordance with the rule of faith. No interpreter can afford to ignore the catholic understanding of the faith, nor can he ignore the work of previous interpreters of the Bible. Origen would have heartily concurred with the Baptist C. H. Spurgeon, who, as we have seen, found it odd that "certain men who talk so much of what the Holy Spirit reveals to themselves, should think so little of what he has revealed to others."[81] Origen was conscious that he had to always check his exegesis against that of other exegetes, with the ultimate source of authority being Scripture itself.[82] In the words of Rowan A. Greer, Origen "consistently argued that the rule of faith and the Scriptures must be used to test his speculations. If they can be demonstrated contrary to these speculations, they must be rejected."[83] Thus, Origen could state in his *Homily on Ezekiel* 7.2: "We have in the sacred Scriptures vessels of silver and gold . . . and when we alter the meaning of Scripture into one which is contrary to the truth, we melt down the words of God and change the things of God into false images."[84]

Third, the exegete must be a person of the Spirit. Only one living in and walking in the Spirit can hope to understand the deep truths that the Spirit has implanted within the scriptural text. For example, in his treatise against Celsus, Origen writes apropos of Psalm 17:12:

> God hides himself as if in darkness from those who cannot bear the radiance of the knowledge of him and who cannot see him partly because of the defilement of the mind that is bound to a human "body of humiliation" [Phil. 3:21], partly because of its restricted capacity to comprehend God. To make it clear that the experience of the knowledge of God comes to men on rare occasions and is to be found by very few people, Moses is said in Scripture to have entered into "the darkness where God was" [Ex. 20:21]. And again of Moses: "Moses alone shall draw near to God; but the others shall not draw near" [Ex. 24:2]. And again that the prophet may show the depth of the doctrines about God, which is unfathomable to people who do not possess the Spirit that searches all things and searches even the deep things of God [1 Cor. 2:10], he says: "The great deep like a garment is his covering" [Ps. 104:6].[85]

[81] *Commenting and Commentaries* (London: Passmore & Alabaster, 1876), 1.
[82] McCartney, "Literal and Allegorical Interpretation," 290–92.
[83] Greer, "Introduction," in his *Origen*, 30.
[84] *Homily on Ezekiel* 7.2. Cited by Bostock, "Allegory and the Interpretation of the Bible," 49.
[85] *Against Celsus* 6.17, in Chadwick, *Origen: Contra Celsum*, 330.

In himself God is light. To men, however, God often appears to be hid in darkness, since their corporeal and finite nature hinders a true comprehension of him. Psalm 104:6 is, for Origen, a clear testimony to the great depth of the knowledge about God that is not plumbed by the majority of men. Some men, like Moses, do receive this knowledge. But it is only through the Spirit, who, according to 1 Corinthians 2:10, searches the depths of God, that any man can hope to be a recipient of such knowledge. Here, 1 Corinthians 2:10 demonstrates the possibility of attaining knowledge of the deeper doctrines about God through the Holy Spirit. For Origen, the source of these deeper doctrines is the Spirit-inspired Scriptures. But since, as we have noted, the Spirit himself has hidden these deeper doctrines beneath the letter of Scripture, only he can reveal them.

A passage from Origen's *Commentary on Matthew* provides an excellent illustration of this hermeneutical principle. Origen is discussing the parable of the unmerciful servant (Matt. 18:23–35) and gives what he considers to be its obvious meaning. Then, after listing those aspects of the parable that probably have a mystical meaning, he adds:

> But it is very likely that a more diligent inquirer would be able to add something more to the number [of details of the parable that have a deeper meaning]. I consider the explication and interpretation [of these details] to be beyond human capacity. The Spirit of Christ is required so that Christ might be understood as he intended. For just as "no one knows the thoughts of a man except the spirit of the man which is in him, and no one knows the thoughts of God except the Spirit of God" [1 Cor. 2:11], so, next to God, no one except the Spirit of Christ knows what has been spoken by Christ in proverbs and parables. The one who partakes [of the Spirit of Christ] not only in so far as the Spirit is of Christ, but also in so far as [the Spirit is] of Christ qua Wisdom and qua Word would be able to contemplate what is revealed to him in that passage.[86]

Only those who have the Spirit of Christ can understand the spiritual meaning of the Scriptures. The exegetes of the church must therefore be highly spiritual persons.

---

[86]*Commentary on Matthew* 14.6 (my translation).

"The Founding Father of Allegory in Christendom"[87]

Having then laid out the parameters within which Origen sought to interpret the Scriptures, let us look at his defense of allegory in *On First Principles* 4.2–3. First of all, in *On First Principles* 4.2.1 he indicates erroneous ways of interpretation. There is what he calls Jewish literalism, which he is convinced leads to unbelief. The early Christian scholar has in mind at this point rabbinic Judaism and its claim that it alone can properly interpret the Old Testament. This form of Judaism was a key aspect of the religious background of Origen's day. More so than any other Christian figure of his day, Origen was acutely aware of Judaism and the Jewish interpretation of the Old Testament. Then, there is a critique of Gnostic exegesis, for Gnostics reject the entire Old Testament, and this leads to theological heresy. Undergirding much of Origen's interpretation is a prevailing anti-Gnostic agenda. And in this regard, he would be aware of critics of allegorization like his fellow North African Tertullian, who argues that "allegories, parables, and riddles" are the chosen method of heretics for explaining away the New Testament.[88] Finally, there is the naïve perspective of "simpler" Christians. Origen does not want his readers to remain on this level, for by maintaining a literalistic reading of Scripture, they will reduce some of the Scriptures to inconsistency and confusion, as we shall see he argues. And such interpretation leads to a scandalous view of God.

Origen then turns to a defense of allegorical interpretation. First of all, he appeals to the example of Paul as found in 1 Corinthians 10:4 and Galatians 4:21–24.[89] Similarly, in *Against Celsus*, Origen appeals to Galatians 4, Ephesians 5:31–32, and selected texts from 1 Corinthians (9:9–10; 10:1–2, 4) to justify the use of allegory. For Origen, therefore, his allegorization has distinct biblical precedent.[90] Further, he notes that the Holy Spirit has woven into the biblical narratives some things that "did not happen" and some that could not have happened, both of which demand an allegorical explanation.[91] Moreover, Origen believes that the Spirit had woven into the Old Testament laws and demands that simply cannot be fulfilled.[92] This is true as well of certain commands in the New Testament. For instance, to take literally the

---

[87]Bostock, "Allegory and the Interpretation of the Bible," 43.
[88]*Scorpiace (Antidote to the Scorpion's Sting)* 11.4.
[89]*On First Principles* 4.2.6.
[90]*Against Celsus* 4.44, 49. He also referred to Pss. 78:2 and 119:18 on occasion.
[91]*On First Principles* 4.2.9; 4.3.1.
[92]*On First Principles* 4.3.2.

command in the Sermon on the Mount to pluck out the right eye if it gives offense (Matt. 5:29) is simply irrational.[93] Through these manifestly "untrue" or "impossible" interpolations the Holy Spirit seeks to prevent the reader from reading the Holy Scripture like other works of world literature, purely for pleasure and thus merely superficially.[94]

The exegete must therefore penetrate through the surface of the holy text into its depths. Origen compares the exegete about this task of discovery to the man who finds the treasure hidden in a field (Matt. 13:44). The true riches are to be found below the surface—in the one case, the surface of the earth; in the other, that of the text.[95] Origen's view of the Bible as a treasure-house of spiritual riches is well seen here. In his *Commentary on Romans* Origen likens the Bible, in the words of Joseph W. Trigg, to "a storehouse in the palace of a rich and powerful king, a place with many different rooms full of gold, silver, precious stones, pearls, purple garments, and diadems."[96]

Moreover, in *De Principiis* 4.2.4, Origen draws upon the classic Greek division of the human person into body, soul, and spirit to argue that Scripture actually operates at three levels: the "bodily," the "soulish," and the "spiritual." Some scholars have argued that Origen's division here corresponds to his reading of Scripture from three different perspectives: the historical, the moral, and the mystical.[97] Others, like Karen Jo Torjesen, have argued that Origen is not giving us here a threefold way of interpreting Scripture. Rather, he is enumerating three classes of hearers—the simple, those more advanced, and those straining toward perfection, the mature (*teleioi*)—as well as three different levels of growth in the individual's reading of the Word of God.[98] The threefoldness in the latter is then a threefoldness in the progression of soul of the student of Scripture. But if this is the case, then it needs to be noted that Origen does not clearly indicate here how one goes from the level of history to the level of the Spirit in interpretation. In the words of Torjesen, instead of "offering us an exegetical hermeneutic of the text, he offers us a pedagogical hermeneutic of the soul."[99] In her analysis of a number of Origen's homilies, Torjesen notes that Origen does structure them along these lines of

---

[93] *On First Principles* 4.3.3.
[94] *On First Principles* 4.2.9.
[95] *On First Principles* 4.3.11.
[96] Joseph W. Trigg, "Introduction" to Hanson, *Allegory and Event*, xxv.
[97] Bostock, "Allegory and the Interpretation of the Bible," 43.
[98] "'Body,' 'Soul,' and 'Spirit' in Origen's Theory of Exegesis," *Anglican Theological Review* 67 (1985): 17–30.
[99] Ibid., 22.

the progression of the soul, usually moving from simpler doctrinal and moral teaching to deeper mysteries of God, some of which he mentions in *On First Principles* 4.2.7, such as the nature of the incarnation and why evil exists.[100] In this sense, then, the goal of exegesis is spiritual formation.

While a modern student of the Bible would not concur with all of Origen's interpretations, this last point seems to be vital. Exegesis has an important spiritual component. The Bible interpreter seeks to understand the text, but this task of interpretation cannot occur in an existential vacuum. While he is reading the text and laboring to understand its meaning and application, the text has its own work to do in shaping the character of the exegete. In fact, it is very evident to anyone who has spent time seriously interacting with Origen's massive exegetical and homiletical corpus that one is dealing with a man of profound spiritual maturity owing to his immersion in the Scriptures, whether or not one agrees with the methods and details of the Egyptian exegete's interpretation.

---

[100]Ibid., 24–29.

Chapter 5

BEING KISSED

The Eucharistic Piety of Cyprian and Ambrose

Let him kiss me with the kisses of his mouth!
For your love is better than wine.

SONG OF SONGS 1:2

In what is the earliest pagan Roman description of Christianity, the imperial governor Pliny the Younger (61/62–ca. 113) mentions, in a letter to the emperor Trajan (r. 98–117), that Christians in Bithynia and Pontus whom he had placed on trial for their beliefs were in the habit of meeting on a weekly basis "to partake of food—but common and harmless food."[1] Pliny's evident surprise that the food consumed by these Christians was both "ordinary and harmless" seems to reveal that he expected to find

---

Most of this chapter is part of a much larger chapter I have written on the Lord's Supper in the ancient church for Thomas R. Schreiner and Matthew Crawford, eds., *The Lord's Supper: Sign of the New Covenant in Christ* (Nashville: Broadman & Holman, forthcoming). Used by permission.

[1] Pliny, *Letter* 10.96. On the date of this letter, see A. N. Sherwin-White, *The Letters of Pliny: A Historical and Social Commentary* (Oxford: Clarendon, 1966), 693. For its interpretation, also see Jorg Christian Salzmann, "Pliny (*ep.* 10, 96) and Christian Liturgy—A Reconsideration," in *Studia Patristica*, ed. Elizabeth A. Livingstone (Louvain: Peeters, 1989), 20:389–95. For an English translation of this letter, see Betty Radice, *The Letters of the Younger Pliny* (Harmondsworth, UK: Penguin, 1963), 293–95.

something quite different, namely, "deviate and sinister meals."[2] Such meals as were supposedly consumed by Christians were luridly described in a mid-second-century speech that some scholars attribute to the Roman grammarian and rhetorician Marcus Cornelius Fronto (ca. 100–166/176) and that was cited by the Christian apologist Minucius Felix (fl. 200–235) in his rebuttal of attacks on the Christian faith:

> The story of their [i.e., Christian] initiation of novices [is] as horrible as it is well known. A baby covered with pastry, so as to deceive the unwary, is set before the initiate in their rites. The novice is encouraged by the pastry crust to give it seemingly harmless jabs and the baby is killed by the unseen and hidden wounds. Thirstily—O for shame!—they lick up his blood, compete in sharing out his limbs, league themselves together by this victim, pledge themselves to mutual silence by this complicity in crime. These rites are fouler than any sacrilege.[3]

Given the number of Christian apologists in the second century who responded to this charge of cannibalism, there seems little doubt that this accusation about Christians was widespread.[4] It is, of course, a garbled misunderstanding of the dominical command to "eat his body" and "drink his blood," as well as mere slander. But if the early Christians were not engaged in such reprehensible deeds, what was actually happening in their assemblies when they took the Lord's Supper? What did they experience as they participated

---

[2]Jakob Engberg, *Impulsore Chresto: Opposition to Christianity in the Roman Empire c. 50–250 AD*, trans. Gregory Carter, Early Christianity in the Context of Antiquity 2 (Frankfurt am Main: Peter Lang GmbH), 188. For a similar opinion, see Albert Henrichs, "Pagan Ritual and the Alleged Crimes of the Early Christians: A Reconsideration," in *Kyriakon: Festschrift Johannes Quasten*, ed. Patrick Granfield and Josef A. Jungmann, 2 vols. (Münster: Verlag Aschendorff, 1970), 1:19–20. For a different reading of this text, see Lautauro Roig Lanzillotta, "The Early Christians and Human Sacrifice," in *The Strange World of Human Sacrifice*, ed. Jan N. Bremmer (Leuven: Peeters, 2007), 84–85.

[3]*Octavius* 9.5, in *Jews and Christians: Graeco-Roman Views*, trans. Molly Whittaker (Cambridge: Cambridge University Press, 1984), 174. For Minucius's rebuttal of this charge, see *Octavius* 30.1–2. Minucius Felix is notoriously difficult to date. For one argument that places his writing *Octavius* during the Severan dynasty, see G. W. Clarke, "The Historical Setting of the *Octavius* of Minucius Felix," *The Journal of Religious History* 4 (1966–67): 265–86. Peter James Cousins argues for a date after 260: "Great Lives in Troubled Times: The Date and Setting of the *Octavius* by Minucius Felix," *Vox Evangelica* 27 (1997): 45–56.

[4]See, for instance, Justin Martyr, *First Apology* 26; Justin Martyr, *Second Apology* 12; Athenagoras, *Plea for the Christians* 3, 35; Theophilus of Antioch, *To Autolycus* 3.4; Tertullian, *Apology* 7.1; Eusebius, *Church History* 5.1. See the excellent and provocative discussions of this issue in Henrichs, "Pagan Ritual and the Alleged Crimes of the Early Christians," 18–35, and Andrew McGowan, "Eating People: Accusations of Cannibalism against Christians in the Second Century," *Journal of Early Christian Studies* 2 (1994): 413–42.

in the Lord's Supper? These are vital questions, for during the course of the Patristic era there is little doubt that the celebration of the Lord's Supper or, as it is more commonly called in this era, the Eucharist became a central aspect of the worship of the church.[5]

In this chapter, we look at the eucharistic thought of two figures in the Latin Patristic tradition, Cyprian of Carthage and Ambrose of Milan, both of whom played key roles in the explication of the meaning of the Lord's Supper and in the development of eucharistic piety.

Cyprian of Carthage

Very little of Cyprian's life prior to his conversion is known. His earliest biographer, a certain Pontius, began his biography at the conversion of Cyprian, for he reckoned that the deeds and character of a man of God ought not to be discussed from any point other than when he was converted.[6] What is known is that Cyprian came from the circles of higher society in Roman North Africa, was accustomed to living in easy circumstances, and, in the words of Patristic scholar Maurice Wiles, "was a man of wealth with a considerable personal fortune."[7] He relinquished much of his wealth at the time of his conversion. Cyprian had won renown and reputation as a rhetor, that is, one who trained aspiring orators and taught the art and science of public discourse. There is no indication that he ever married.

By the early 240s, Cyprian became increasingly disillusioned with his world, and the luxuries and privileges he possessed came to hold little appeal for him.[8] He was drawn to the Christian faith through his friendship with a certain Caecilianus, an aged elder in the Christian community at Carthage. What made him decide to become a Christian? One author has suggested that he was disgusted at the world in which he lived.[9] There is certainly evidence of that in a letter he wrote shortly after his conversion,[10] but this same letter clearly indicates that there was a key personal element that led

---

[5]Daniel Sheerin, "Eucharistic Liturgy," in *The Oxford Handbook of Early Christian Studies*, ed. Susan Ashbrook Harvey and David G. Hunter (Oxford: Oxford University Press, 2008), 723.
[6]*Life of Cyprian* 2. On Cyprian's life and thought, see especially Peter Hinchliff, *Cyprian of Carthage and the Unity of the Christian Church* (London: Geoffrey Chapman, 1974); Michael M. Sage, *Cyprian*, Patristic Monograph Series 1 (Philadelphia: Philadelphia Patristic Foundation, 1975); J. Patout Burns, *Cyprian the Bishop* (London: Routledge, 2002); and Burns, "Cyprian of Carthage," *The Expository Times* 120 (2009): 469–77.
[7]"The Theological Legacy of St Cyprian," in his *Working Papers in Doctrine* (London: SCM, 1976), 68.
[8]See Cyprian, *Letter to Donatus* 3–4.
[9]See Hinchliff, *Cyprian of Carthage*, 26.
[10]*Letter to Donatus* 6–14.

Cyprian to become a Christian. As he heard the gospel, he became convicted of his sins, among which he noted pride, anger, covetousness, and lust.[11] He sought to reform his life, but to no avail. Thinking that he would never be able to divest himself of these sins, he despaired of ever living a life of virtue and plunged back into his old ways.[12] But then—and he does not tell us the details—he was suddenly converted, and, in his words, "immediately in a marvelous manner doubtful matters clarified themselves, the closed opened, the shadowy shone with light, what seemed impossible was able to be accomplished."[13] Looking back on this time of transformation, Cyprian was later aware that it was the Holy Spirit who had brought him to faith and the new birth: "Our power is of God, I say, all of it is of God. From him we have life."[14]

And so Cyprian became a catechumen, a learner in the Christian faith. Most catechumens in the church at Carthage would have been drawn from poorer classes. As a member of the upper class, Cyprian undoubtedly would have stood out. Yet, of all the various groups and subcultures within the empire, the church was virtually the only one that drew its membership from across the social and economic spectrum and managed to weld them into a genuine community.[15]

Within a couple of years of his conversion and baptism in 245/246, Cyprian was appointed bishop of Carthage, which made him the leading bishop in Latin-speaking Africa and an influential voice in the development of North African Christianity.[16] Although initially opposed by more senior elders in Carthage because of his too-rapid advance to the episcopate and the fact that he seemed to be still too much the secular Roman patron dispensing favors to his clients, Cyprian proved to be, in the empire-wide persecutions of the late 240s and 250s, a wise and balanced Christian leader. He was martyred during the reign of the emperor Valerian for refusing to perform ritual sacrifice to the Roman gods.[17]

---

[11] *Letter to Donatus* 6–14.

[12] *Letter to Donatus* 4.

[13] *Letter to Donatus* 4, in *Saint Cyprian: Treatises*, trans. Roy J. Deferrari (New York: Fathers of the Church, 1958), 10.

[14] *Letter to Donatus* 4, in Deferrari, *Saint Cyprian: Treatises*, 10. Though brief and compact, Cyprian's account of his conversion has some of the very same emphases as the much more famous conversion narrative from the ancient church, namely, that of Augustine.

[15] Hinchliff, *Cyprian of Carthage*, 28–29.

[16] Burns, "Cyprian of Carthage," 469.

[17] See *The Acts of St. Cyprian*, in *The Acts of the Christian Martyrs*, ed. Herbert Musurillo (Oxford: Clarendon, 1972), 168–75.

"Your Cup Is Intoxicating": Cyprian on the Eucharist

The "first authentic eucharistic treatise" in the pre-Constantinian era is the way Cyprian's *Letter* 63 has been described.[18] It was written to Caecilius, bishop of Biltha,[19] probably in the autumn of 253,[20] to address the error of an aquarian Eucharist, that is, the use of water alone instead of a mixture of wine and water in the Lord's Supper.[21] Cyprian begins with the basic principle that Christians are not at liberty to change "what the Lord Jesus Christ did and taught" unless they want to offend their Master.[22] When it comes to the eucharistic cup, this specifically means that "the chalice that is offered in memory of him should be offered mixed with wine. For since Christ pronounces: 'I am the true vine,' the blood of Christ without qualification is not water."[23] Christ's own use of wine at the Last Supper as an illustration of his blood instructs the church that "the chalice should be mixed by commingling water and wine."[24] And this is what was handed down by the apostles. To use water alone is thus to go against domini-cal, "evangelical and apostolic practice."[25] The Carthaginian bishop finds support for his argument from various Old Testament examples that he regards as types[26] of the passion of Christ and its representation in the bread and the wine: the inebriation of Noah,[27] the offering of bread and wine by

---

[18] A. Hamman, "Eucharist. I. In the Fathers," in *Encyclopedia of the Early Church*, ed. Angelo Di Berardino, trans. Adrian Walford (New York: Oxford University Press, 1992), 1:293; Daniel J. Sheerin, *The Eucharist*, Message of the Fathers of the Church 7 (Wilmington, DE: Michael Glazier, 1986), 256.

[19] For the few details known about Caecilius, see Edward White Benson, "Caecilius (6) Bishop of Biltha," in *A Dictionary of Christian Biography*, ed. William Smith and Henry Wace (Boston: Little, Brown, and Co., 1877), 1:369, col. 2.

[20] For the date of the letter, see Sage, *Cyprian*, 291, 366; and Sheerin, *Eucharist*, 256.

[21] For this issue, see Alvah Hovey, "Patristic Testimonies as to Wine, Especially as Used in the Lord's Supper," *The Baptist Quarterly Review* 10 (1888): 78–93; G. W. Clarke, *The Letters of St. Cyprian of Carthage*, Ancient Christian Writers 46 (New York: Newman, 1986), 3:288–90; Andrew McGowan, *Ascetic Eucharists: Food and Drink in Early Christian Ritual Meals* (Oxford: Clarendon, 1999), passim and especially 204–11; Margaret M. Daly-Denton, "Water in the Eucharistic Cup: A Feature of the Eucharist in Johannine Trajectories through Early Christianity," *Irish Theological Quarterly* 72 (2007): 356–70.

[22] *Letter* 63.1, in *St Cyprian of Carthage: On the Church: Select Letters*, trans. Allen Brent (Crestwood, NY: St Vladimir's Seminary Press, 2006), 173; hereafter this translation will be cited as Brent, *St Cyprian*.

[23] *Letter* 63.2, in Brent, *St Cyprian*, 173, altered. The quote is from John 15:1. See also *Letter* 63.10, 14, 16, 18. In *Letter* 63.18 Cyprian cites Matt. 28:18–20 to buttress his appeal to dominical authority and by implication includes the use of water and wine in the Lord's Supper as one of the things that Christ commanded his apostles to teach to disciples.

[24] *Letter* 63.9, in Brent, *St Cyprian*, 179.

[25] *Letter* 63.11, in Brent, *St Cyprian*, 180.

[26] Cyprian uses the term *sacramentum*, that is, "pledge" or "sign," to describe these examples.

[27] This is a most curious type, which led Edward White Benson to speak about the "wildness ... of the Biblical interpretations and the looseness of the logic" in Cyprian's letter. See his *Cyprian: His*

Melchizedek, Lady Wisdom in Proverbs 9, the blessing of Judah, and an Isaianic prediction of the Messiah in Isaiah 63.[28] Cyprian then notes that it is the initiatory rite of baptism that is "in water alone."[29] The Eucharist, though, must employ both water and wine, for its purpose is to recall the shedding of Christ's blood.

Cyprian also buttresses his argument with a phrase from Psalm 23:5 as it appeared in the Old Latin translation of the Psalms. In the version of this psalm known to Cyprian, there was a statement, "Your cup, though the finest, is intoxicating" (*calix tuus inebrians perquam optimus*), which the bishop interprets as a reference to the Lord's Supper.[30] As Cyprian notes, water alone never causes inebriation. For drunkenness to occur, there must be wine. Of course, partaking of the cup in the Eucharist produces an insobriety entirely different from that of this world's wine. Eucharistic insobriety makes men and women "sober, in the sense that it restores hearts back to a spiritual wisdom, in the sense that each person returns to his senses about his understanding of God from tasting the experience of this age."[31] What is fascinating about this interpretation is that it provides us with a vantage point to reflect upon the richness of Cyprian's experience of the Lord's Table.

For the North African theologian, the Lord's Supper is a place of spiritual wisdom, for it helps to recall men and women from their temptation of being infatuated with the world. As Cyprian goes on to note, "drinking the blood of the Lord and his saving cup" is a means of forgetting this world's pattern of living. And just as "ordinary wine" initially has a relaxing effect and a way of dispelling sadness, so it is that the Lord's Supper, conducted as the Lord directed—which, in this context, means wine

---

Life, His Times, His Work (London: Macmillan, 1897), 291. And yet the overall thrust of Cyprian's typological exegesis here is common to the Fathers, namely, "to situate Christ himself within the sacred narratives of the past in the sense that he both participates in and fulfills those narratives" (John J. O'Keefe and R. R. Reno, *Sanctified Vision: An Introduction to Early Christian Interpretation of the Bible* [Baltimore: Johns Hopkins University Press, 2005], 73). Like most precritical exegetes, Cyprian was eager to discover what any given biblical passage meant for him and the believing community of his day.

[28] *Letter* 63.3–7. For a discussion of various aspects of Cyprian's typological exegesis, see Clarke, *Letters of St. Cyprian*, 3:292–94. For a listing of other types of the Lord's Supper found by the Fathers in the Old Testament, see Sheerin, "Eucharistic Liturgy," 723.

[29] *Letter* 63.8, in Brent, *St Cyprian*, 177.

[30] *Letter* 63.11, in Brent, *St Cyprian*, 180. For the Latin, see J.-P. Migne, ed., *Patrologiae cursus completus . . . Series prima* [latina] (Paris, 1844), 4.382b; hereafter, *Patrologia latina*.

[31] *Letter* 63.11, in Brent, *St Cyprian*, 180. The theme of *sobria ebrietas* was a favorite one with the Fathers. See below for its development by Ambrose.

mixed with water—relieves the believer of those "choking sins" that had overwhelmed him or her. The Eucharist is thus a place where the believer knows afresh the forgiveness of the Lord and as a result is suffused with joy.[32] In relation to this, elsewhere Cyprian can encourage Christians as "soldiers of Christ" to drink "the cup of the blood of Christ" so that they might be enabled to renounce the world even to the point of shedding their blood for Christ.[33]

The Eucharist also speaks of the union of the people with their Lord. Cyprian suggests that the water in the cup represents the people of God, while wine, of course, is indicative of the shed blood of the Savior. When the water is mixed with wine in the cup, then, it depicts the unbreakable union of love that Christians have with one another and with their Lord. Given what the cup therefore represents, it is improper to use either water alone or wine by itself. Similarly, the bread that is broken consists of "wheat gathered and ground down and kneaded together" with water to form one loaf. For Cyprian, the Eucharist is a powerful experiential witness to the "sworn bond" (*sacramentum*) that binds together believers as one body in Christ.[34] This was especially important for Cyprian as he sought to deal with schismatics in the North African churches who refused to offer full restoration to those who had apostatized in the Decian persecution (249–251) and who, afterward, were sincerely repentant.[35] As J. Patout Burns notes, for Cyprian, the "uniting of the community in Christ became the major function of the Eucharist."[36]

This letter is also noteworthy for it contains, in the estimation of the incisive Congregationalist theologian P. T. Forsyth (1848–1921), "an absolutely unscriptural change." After linking the biblical affirmation about the offering of Christ, the high priest of God, "as a sacrifice to the Father" with his command to his disciples to celebrate the Lord's Supper in his remembrance, Cyprian concludes that Jesus is asking his disciples to do exactly as he did. This means that the one presiding at the Eucharist "imitates that

---

[32] *Letter* 63.11, in Brent, *St Cyprian*, 181.

[33] *Letter* 58.1–2. I owe this reference to Andrew McGowan, "Rethinking Agape and Eucharist in Early North African Christianity," *Studia Liturgica* 34 (2004): 175. On this passage, see also John D. Laurance, *"Priest" as Type of Christ: The Leader of the Eucharist in Salvation History according to Cyprian of Carthage,* American University Studies 7, vol. 5 (New York: Peter Lang, 1984), 185–88.

[34] *Letter* 63.13, in Brent, *St Cyprian*, 181–82.

[35] For a helpful outline of this persecution and its impact on the churches in North Africa and Rome, see Brent, "Introduction," in *St Cyprian*, 17–38.

[36] Burns, "Cyprian of Carthage," 474. See also Alan Kreider, "Worship and Evangelism in Pre-Christendom (The Laing Lecture 1994)," *Vox Evangelica* 24 (1994): 23: "The eucharist was a unitive rite . . ."

which Christ did," when he "offers a true and full sacrifice in the Church to God the Father."[37] In making this exegetical move, Cyprian becomes, according to Forsyth, "the chief culprit in effecting the change from a *sacrificium laudis* [a sacrifice of praise] by the Church to a *sacrificium propitiatorium* [a propitiatory sacrifice] by the priest."[38] Whether or not Forsyth is right to designate Cyprian as the "chief culprit" in this regard is moot.[39] Earlier authors, such as Justin Martyr and Irenaeus of Lyons, had also used the term "sacrifice" with regard to the Eucharist, based on their exegesis of Malachi 1:11.[40] However, whereas they saw the people of God corporately offering up the sacrifice of the Eucharist in purity of heart, Cyprian identifies the bishop or minister as the one who is uniquely called to do this and who, in this aspect of his ministry, imitates the high priestly sacrifice of Christ himself.[41] Fundamental to this shift in focus is Cyprian's use of the term "priest" (*sacerdos*) as a description of the one presiding at the Eucharist. Prior to Cyprian, this term was never used to designate Christian ministry per se, but Cyprian, as in the letter under consideration, continually calls the one presiding at the Eucharist, whether bishop or elder, a *sacerdos*.[42] And just as there are types of Christ's passion in the history of God's people preceding the incarnation, as Cyprian outlines in this letter, so in the history of the church since the death and resurrection of Christ there are priests who imitate Christ's priesthood and who are vehicles for his presence in the church's worship.[43]

Cyprian well represents certain shifts in eucharistic thought and praxis that are taking place during the third century. For him, the Eucharist is a pledge of the unity of the body of Christ as it battles schism in the midst of empire-wide persecution. He also reaffirms the centrality of the table for Christian experiential piety by using the image of "sober intoxication" as a summary way of describing the experience of eating the bread and drinking the wine. In a distinct break from earlier perspectives, though, Cyprian employs the term "priest" (*sacerdos*) to describe the one presiding at the table,

---

[37] *Letter* 63.14, in Brent, *St Cyprian*, 183–84.

[38] *The Church and the Sacraments*, 4th ed. (London: Independent, 1953), 272. Also see E. Glenn Hinson, "The Lord's Supper in Early Church History," *Review and Expositor* 64 (1969): 18–19.

[39] See Alasdair I. C. Heron, *Table and Tradition* (Philadelphia: Westminster Press, 1983), 75–76, for similar statements by Tertullian and Origen.

[40] See Justin Martyr, *Dialogue with Trypho* 41; Irenaeus of Lyons, *Against Heresies* 4.17.4–4.18.3.

[41] Heron, *Table and Tradition*, 76.

[42] Laurance, *"Priest" as Type of Christ*, 195–200.

[43] Ibid., 223–30.

which would provide ground for later, strongly sacerdotal, interpretations of the Lord's Supper.

Ambrose of Milan

The public embrace of Christianity by a Roman emperor, namely Flavius Valerius Constantinus, otherwise known as Constantine I, in the second decade of the fourth century AD had such far-reaching effects that, by the time he died, there was scarcely any facet of the public life of the empire or that of the church that was not impacted by his policy of official Christianization. Constantine genuinely perceived himself to be a friend and ally of the church who was used by God to bring an end to the imperial persecution of God's people.[44] Yet, the long-term impact of his reign on Christianity was not always for the best. For instance, not long after Constantine's death, his son, the Arian emperor Constantius II (317–361), was persecuting supporters of the Nicene Creed, such as Athanasius, and thus setting a precedent for the later extensive involvement of the state in the life of the church.

Among the key defenders of Nicene orthodoxy in the West against Arian-instigated persecution was Ambrose, an aristocrat like Cyprian and a provincial governor before being appointed bishop of Milan in 374.[45] With little theological education and not even baptized, Ambrose was called by the congregation in Milan to be their bishop following the death of his Arian predecessor, Auxentius. Used to the exercise of power, Ambrose did not find it easy to adjust to his new role, and his relationships with those like the Arian empress Justina (d. 388) or the decidedly orthodox Theodosius I (347–395), who made Nicene Trinitarianism the official religion of the Roman Empire, illustrate the dangers faced by influential church leaders in a society now committed to the Christian faith.[46] Ambrose strongly encouraged young Christians to embrace a life of virginity and wrote his first theological

---

[44] For a convincing argument in this regard, see Timothy D. Barnes, *Constantine and Eusebius* (Cambridge, MA: Harvard University Press, 1981).

[45] On the life and thought of Ambrose, see Daniel H. Williams, *Ambrose of Milan and the End of the Nicene-Arian Conflicts* (Oxford: Clarendon; New York: Oxford University Press, 1995); and Ivor Davidson, "Ambrose" in *The Early Christian World*, ed. Philip F. Esler (London: Routledge, 2000), 2:1175–1204. For selections of his writings, see Boniface Ramsey, *Ambrose* (London: Routledge, 1997). The classic study is F. Holmes Dudden, *The Life and Times of St. Ambrose*, 2 vols. (Oxford: Clarendon, 1935).

[46] As Ramsey notes, "Ambrose was above all a man of the spirit, whose activities in the public forum were guided overwhelmingly by spiritual considerations, however ill conceived they occasionally were. It is impossible . . . not to posit a deep spirituality in a man in whose writings the mystical meaning of

treatise on this subject. His preaching was deeply influenced by the allegorical exegesis of Origen, which we looked at in the previous chapter. It was
in fact his use of allegorization that encouraged Augustine to pay attention to his exposition of Christianity and thus contributed to Augustine's
conversion.[47] Augustine also makes mention of Ambrose's introduction of
congregational hymn singing to the church at Milan.[48] Ambrose himself
wrote a number of hymns that helped lay a foundation for Latin hymnody.
Although Ambrose was not a brilliant theologian, his deep knowledge of
Greek gave him access to the riches of the Greek Patristic tradition, which
he passed on to the West through his various works. Ivor Davidson rightly
notes that Ambrose's role in the formation of Latin Christianity was both
"remarkable and complex."[49] This is clearly the case with regard to eucharistic
thought and piety, where Ambrose was a pioneer of new ways of thinking
about the Lord's Supper.[50]

Being Kissed by Christ: Ambrose's Eucharistic Piety

The heart of Ambrose's eucharistic thought and reflection is to be found
in his *On the Sacraments* and *On the Mysteries*. Like Cyprian, Ambrose sees
prefigurations of the Eucharist in such Old Testament texts as the Genesis
account of Melchizedek's offering bread and wine to Abraham.[51] Again, like
Cyprian and other earlier authors, Ambrose uses realistic language about the
bread and wine: when consumed in the Lord's Supper they are the body and
blood of Christ.[52] He goes beyond earlier authors, however, by identifying
Christ's words of institution as the means by which a change is effected in
the elements of bread and wine.

> Before [the bread] is consecrated, it is bread; but when Christ's words have
> been added, it is the body of Christ. Finally, hear him as he says: "Take and
> eat of this, all of you; for this is my body" [cf. Matt. 26:26–27]. And before

---

the Song of Songs plays so prominent a role, and who was capable of composing such extraordinary
hymns" (*Ambrose*, x).

[47]See Augustine, *Confessions* 6.3–4.

[48]*Confessions* 9.7.

[49]Davidson, "Ambrose," 1175.

[50]Raymond Johanny, *L'Eucharistie, centre de l'histoire du salut chez saint Ambroise de Milan* (Paris:
Beauchesne, 1968); Davidson, "Ambrose," 1197; Gary Macy, *The Theologies of the Eucharist in the Early
Scholastic Period: A Study of the Salvific Function of the Sacrament according to the Theologians c. 1080–
c. 1220* (Oxford: Clarendon, 1984), 19.

[51]*On the Sacraments* 4.3.10–12; 5.1.1; *On the Mysteries* 8.45–46.

[52]*On the Sacraments* 4.4.14, 19–20.

the words of Christ, the chalice is full of wine and water; when the words of Christ have been added, then blood is effected [*efficitur*], which redeemed the people. So behold in what great respects the expression of Christ is able to change [*convertere*] all things.[53]

Fourth-century theologians were generally more explicit than previous authors in spelling out details of the changes that happen to the bread and the wine at the celebration of the Lord's Supper.[54] For a Greek-speaking author like Cyril of Jerusalem, it is the prayer for the descent of the Spirit upon the elements that brings about a change in them.[55] The West, on the other hand, would follow Ambrose in locating the power to effect change in the elements in the words of Christ.[56] To those who found the idea of such a change hard to believe, Ambrose brought forward a whole array of biblical examples, from Moses' rod, which was changed into a serpent and back again, to Elijah's iron axe head being made able to float.[57] Ambrose is able to avoid a crass materialistic interpretation of the changes that take place in the elements by emphasizing that

Christ is in that sacrament, because it is the body of Christ; therefore it is not bodily food, but spiritual. Whence also the Apostle says of the type of it that "our fathers ate spiritual meat, and drank spiritual drink" [1 Cor. 10:3–4]. For the body of God is a spiritual body; the body of Christ is the body of a divine Spirit, because Christ is Spirit [cf. 1 Cor. 15:45; 2 Cor. 3:17].[58]

---

[53] *On the Sacraments* 4.5.23, in *Saint Ambrose: Theological and Dogmatic Works*, trans. Roy J. Deferrari, The Fathers of the Church 44 (Washington, DC: The Catholic University of America Press, 1963), 305. See also Ambrose, *On the Sacraments* 4.4.14, 19; *On the Mysteries* 52.

[54] R. J. Halliburton, "The Patristic Theology of the Eucharist," in *The Study of Liturgy*, ed. Cheslyn Jones, Geoffrey Wainwright, and Edward Yarnold (London: SPCK, 1978), 207; Everett Ferguson, "The Lord's Supper in Church History: The Early Church Through the Medieval Period," in *The Lord's Supper: Believers Church Perspectives*, ed. Dale R. Stoffer (Scottdale, PA; Waterloo, ON: Herald, 1997), 28.

[55] See, for example, Cyril of Jerusalem, *On the Mysteries* 5.7. For discussion of this text, see Heron, *Table and Tradition*, 66; Ferguson, "Lord's Supper in Church History," 28–29.

[56] Heron, *Table and Tradition*, 66–67.

[57] *On the Sacraments* 4.4.11; *On the Mysteries* 51–52.

[58] *On the Mysteries* 9.58, in *St Ambrose, On the Sacraments and On the Mysteries*, trans. T. Thompson, ed. J. H. Srawley (London: S.P.C.K., 1950), 150. See also the comments of C. W. Dugmore, "Sacrament and Sacrifice in the Early Fathers," *The Journal of Ecclesiastical History* 2 (1951): 35–36; G. W. H. Lampe, "The Eucharist in the Thought of the Early Church," in Lampe et al., *Eucharistic Theology Then and Now* (London: S.P.C.K., 1968), 52–53.

Nevertheless, he can still say that in the mystery of the Lord's Supper believers adore the flesh of Christ, which might lead to confusion between the bread and the wine and that which they signified.[59]

Ambrose is also a pioneer in one other important area relating to the Eucharist, namely, the use of the Song of Songs to express the believer's experience at the table.[60] It is Christ, Ambrose remarks, who calls the believer, cleansed of sin, to come to his "marvelous sacraments" with the words "Let him kiss me with the kiss of his mouth" (Song of Songs 1:2), which Ambrose interprets to mean, "Let Christ impress a kiss upon me."[61] The reception of the Lord's Supper is here likened to the joyous experience of being kissed by one's beloved. This loving communion that Christ has with his people through the Eucharist Ambrose further likens to the beloved coming into his garden and drinking his wine with milk (Song of Songs 5:1). This is nothing less, Ambrose maintains, than Christ giving his people forgiveness of sins through the supper and their subsequent rejoicing or inebriation in the Spirit.[62] To be so inebriated with the Spirit, Ambrose continues, is to be "deeply rooted in Christ" and as such is a state that Ambrose can only describe as "a glorious inebriation" (*praeclara ebrietas*).[63]

Along with the significant changes that came into the life of the church and its worship in the fourth century with the toleration of Christianity, there came a movement toward more exact specification of how the bread and the wine served as the body and blood of Christ. In the East, Cyril of Jerusalem appears to have been the first to specify the details of this conversion, though the greatest influence in this regard came from Gregory of Nyssa, the brother of Basil of Caesarea, whom we will look at in the next chapter. In the West, Ambrose is the main conduit of this line of thinking. Ambrose's emphasis on the transformation of the bread and the wine into the body and blood of Christ would increasingly make the Lord's Supper not so much a community celebration, as it was for earlier Christians, but a

---

[59] *On the Holy Spirit* 3.79.

[60] Hamman, "Eucharist. I. In the Fathers," 1:293. The employment of the Song of Songs as an expression of eucharistic piety would come to full fruition much later in the writings of such medieval authors as Bernard of Clairvaux (1090–1153) and Puritan pastors like Edward Taylor (1642–1729).

[61] *On the Sacraments* 5.2.5–7.

[62] *On the Sacraments* 5.3.15–17 (Patrologia latina 16.449a–c).

[63] *On the Sacraments* 5.3.17 (Patrologia latina 16.449c–450a).

place of adoration, reverent awe, and fear lest something be done wrong.[64] Ambrose's thought would also inexorably lead to a confusion of symbol and meaning. His use of the Song of Songs, however, tempered both of these developments, for by it Christians were reminded that the table was ultimately meant to be a place of exuberant spiritual joy over sins forgiven and union with Christ.

---

[64]Macy, *Theologies of the Eucharist*, 19–20; Lampe, "Eucharist in the Thought of the Early Church," 52.

Chapter 6

BEING HOLY AND RENOUNCING THE WORLD

The Experience of Basil of Caesarea

*To those who by patience in well-doing seek for glory
and honor and immortality, he will give eternal life.*

ROMANS 2:7

We know more about Basil of Caesarea than about any other Christian of the ancient church apart from Augustine of Hippo. Central to our knowledge of Basil's life is a marvelous collection of 311 letters,[1] as well as two panegyrics that come from men who were extremely

---

Portions of this chapter have appeared in print as "Defending the Holy Spirit's Deity: Basil of Caesarea, Gregory of Nyssa, and the Pneumatomachian Controversy of the 4th Century," *The Southern Baptist Journal of Theology* 7, no. 3 (Fall 2003): 74–79; and "'Strive for Glory with God': Some Reflections by Basil of Caesarea on Humility," *The Gospel Witness* 82, no. 3 (September 2003): 3–6. Both used by permission.

[1] Anthony Meredith, *The Cappadocians* (Crestwood, NY: St Vladimir's Seminary Press, 1995), 20. There are 368 letters attributed to Basil, of which we know that some 57 were not written by him. See P. J. Fedwick, "New Editions and Studies of the Works of Basil of Caesarea," in *Paideia Cristiana: Studi in onore di Mario Naldini* (Rome: Gruppo Editoriale Internazionale, 1994), 616–17. For a chronology of Basil's life and all of his works, see, Paul Jonathan Fedwick, *The Church and the Charisma of Leadership in Basil of Caesarea* (Toronto: Pontifical Institute of Mediaeval Studies,

close to him, his friend Gregory of Nazianzus and his (Basil's) younger brother Gregory of Nyssa.

Early Years and Conversion

Basil was born in Caesarea, then the capital of Cappadocia (now in central Turkey), around the year 330.[2] The families of both his father and mother, Basil and Emmelia, had suffered for the Christian faith during the persecution of Diocletian. Basil's maternal grandfather had been martyred, while his paternal grandparents had spent seven years hiding in the forests of Pontus during this most vicious of imperial persecutions.[3] As Philip Rousseau notes, Basil's world was filled with men and women who were "children of confessors and children of martyrs."[4] The property of both families was confiscated by the state, but by the time of Basil's birth, his immediate family was prosperous and owned a number of properties throughout Cappadocia and Pontus.

Basil's early education came from his father. Upon his father's death in 340, Basil went to study at Caesarea, where he met and formed a lifelong friendship with Gregory of Nazianzus. Further studies followed at Constantinople, and then it was on to Athens in the 350s, where he and Nazianzen studied rhetoric together. Many years later Nazianzen fondly recalled their life together as students.

> In studies, in lodgings, in discussions I had him as companion. . . . We had all things in common. . . . But above all it was God, of course, and a mutual desire for higher things, that drew us to each other. As a result we reached such a pitch of confidence that we revealed the depths of our hearts, becoming ever more united in our yearning.[5]

1979), 133–55. For a complete bibliography of works on Basil, see Fedwick, *Bibliotheca Basiliana Universalis: A Study of the Manuscript Tradition, Translations and Editions of the Works of Basil of Caesarea*, vol. 5, *Studies of Basil of Caesarea and His World: An Annotated Bio-Bibliography* (Turnhout: Brepols, 2004).

[2]For an excellent study of Basil, see especially Fedwick, *The Church and the Charisma of Leadership in Basil of Caesarea*. Also see the biographical sketch in Stephen M. Hildebrand, *The Trinitarian Theology of Basil of Caesarea: A Synthesis of Greek Thought and Biblical Truth* (Washington, DC: The Catholic University of America Press, 2007), 18–29.

[3]Gregory of Nazianzus, *Oration* 43.6.

[4]Philip Rousseau, *Basil of Caesarea* (Berkeley: University of California Press, 1998), 6.

[5]*On His Life* 2.225–36, in *Saint Gregory of Nazianzus: Three Poems*, trans. Denis Molaise Meehan, The Fathers of the Church 75 (Washington, DC: The Catholic University of America Press, 1987), 83–84.

Given this estimation of friendship, it is no surprise that Gregory would state, "If anyone were to ask me, 'What is the best thing in life?,' I would answer, 'Friends.'"[6]

Although Basil deeply appreciated his friendship with Gregory, he rarely referred to his time in Athens in his later writings. In an early letter, written probably to the man who would become his mentor, Eustathius of Sebaste (ca. 300–ca. 377), Basil could say he had left Athens, "scorning everything there."[7] And in an undated sermon he called the city "a school of impurity," which might be a reference to the fact that the city's learning had a tendency to lead to heresy.[8] One of the problems that education in Athens posed for Basil—with its stress on rhetorical display—is that it seemed to run counter to the simplicity that should accompany Christian speech. Thus, Basil stressed in a letter to Diodore of Tarsus (d. ca. 390) that a "simple and unlaboured style" befits "the purpose of a Christian, who writes not so much for display as for general edification."[9] And he could say in his sermon on humility, "If the wisdom which is from God be lacking, these acquisitions [of human wisdom and sagacity] are worthless" and "the profit of human wisdom is illusory."[10]

In 355 or 356 Basil cut short his studies to return home and become a teacher of rhetoric, as his father had been. His elder sister Macrina, however, who had been strongly influenced by the monasticism of Eustathius, challenged him to give his life unreservedly to Christ.[11] It was in that same year that Basil was converted. In his own words:

> I wasted nearly all of my youth in the vain labor that occupied me in the acquisition of the teachings of that wisdom which God has made foolish. Then at last, as if roused from a deep sleep, I looked at the wonderful light of the truth of the gospel, and I perceived the worthlessness of the wisdom of the rulers of this age, who are doomed to destruction. After I had mourned

---

[6] Cited by Carolinne White, *Christian Friendship in the Fourth Century* (Cambridge: Cambridge University Press, 1992), 70.

[7] *Letter* 1, in *Saint Basil: The Letters*, trans. Roy J. Deferrari, 4 vols. (1926–1934; repr., Cambridge, MA: Harvard University Press, 1972), 1:3.

[8] So Rousseau, *Basil of Caesarea*, 40, interprets it.

[9] *Letter* 135.1, in Deferrari, *Saint Basil: The Letters*, 2:307. For further discussion of this subject in Basil, see Rousseau, *Basil of Caesarea*, 44–60.

[10] *Homily* 20.2, in *Saint Basil: Ascetical Works*, trans. M. Monica Wagner (New York: Fathers of the Church, 1950), 477, 478; hereafter this translation will be cited as Wagner, *Ascetical Works*. And yet, Basil's *Hexaemeron* (*Homilies on the Six Days of Creation*) reveals a wide familiarity with the scientific knowledge of his day, which he would have acquired at Athens. See Meredith, *Cappadocians*, 21.

[11] See Gregory of Nyssa, *The Life of Saint Macrina*, trans. Kevin Corrigan (2001; repr., Eugene, Oregon: Wipf & Stock, 2005), 26.

deeply for my miserable life, I prayed that guidance be given to me for my introduction to the precepts of piety.[12]

A Monastic Reformer

Basil's conversion to Christ was also a conversion to a monastic lifestyle. Monasticism had become an increasingly popular form of Christian discipleship after the acclamation of Constantine I as emperor in 306 at York. Constantine claimed to be a Christian and certainly loaded favors upon the church once he had secured control of the entire Western Roman Empire in 312.[13] As Christianity became the government's preferred religion during his thirty-one years in power and then increasingly the only religious option during the reigns of his Christian successors, many were tempted to join the church simply because it provided a way to get ahead in society. In other words, during the fourth and fifth centuries nominal believers entered the church in significantly large numbers to bring about an identity crisis within the church. In essence that crisis can be boiled down to this question: What does it mean to be a Christian in a "Christian" society? As we saw in chapters 2–4, during the second and third centuries the lines between the church and Graeco-Roman society were fairly sharply drawn. And in a certain sense, the bodies of the martyrs were the boundaries of the church. But after Constantine the lines of demarcation became completely blurred. The answer to this crisis of ecclesial identity was the renewal movement that we call monasticism. In the long run this movement created as many problems as it set out to solve, but in the fourth century, in the hands of such capable exponents as Athanasius and Basil of Caesarea, it did indeed function as a vehicle of renewal. In fact, it played an essential role in the survival of Christianity after the fall of the Western Roman Empire, for it was in the monastic sodalities formed by this renewal movement, for instance, that the Christian Scriptures were preserved and handed on.

The first form of monasticism was eremitic, located in the deserts of Egypt and Syria, and inspired by the life of Antony (ca. 251–356), a life lived largely

---

[12]*Letter* 223.2 (my translation).

[13]For analysis of Constantine's religious motivation, see especially Hermann Doerries, *Constantine the Great*, trans. Roland H. Bainton (New York: Harper and Row, 1972); Timothy D. Barnes, *Constantine and Eusebius* (Cambridge, MA: Harvard University Press, 1981); Paul Keresztes, "Constantine: Called by Divine Providence," in *Studia Patristica*, ed. Elizabeth A. Livingstone (Kalamazoo, MI: Cistercian, 1985), 18/1:47–53; the essays in Noel Lenski, ed., *The Cambridge Companion to the Age of Constantine* (Cambridge: Cambridge University Press, 2006); and Paul Stephenson, *Constantine: Unconquered Emperor, Christian Victor* (London: Quercus, 2009).

in solitude and marked by prayer, asceticism, and combat with demonic powers. Basil, on the other hand, would be a pioneer of coenobitic monasticism—a monasticism centered on living the Christian life together with others who were like-minded. And while Basil never entertained the view that the monastic lifestyle was for every believer, he did believe that in fourth-century Graeco-Roman society, where Christianity was fast becoming the only tolerated religion and where many were now flocking into the church for base motives, monasticism was a needed force for church renewal. In time, during the 360s, Basil became a leading figure in the establishment of monastic communities, which he sought to model after the experience of the Jerusalem church as it is depicted in the early chapters of Acts.

Not long after his conversion Basil was baptized, a deeply moving experience for Basil and one that had profound ramifications for his theology, as we shall see. In 356/357,[14] Basil left for a tour of the ascetic communities of Mesopotamia, Syria, Palestine, and Egypt, many of which, at first glance, appear to have impressed him deeply. We find him writing such phrases as "I admired," "I was amazed," and "all this moved my admiration." Yet, it is interesting to note that Basil never contemplated joining the Egyptian and Syrian monks. Nor did he, upon returning home, attempt to imitate their ascetic exploits. Why not, if he appears to have admired them so greatly? His trip showed him some of the problems of the monastic movement, notably its tendency toward spiritual elitism and egoism, and its failure to cultivate a spirit of humility and love for one's neighbor. Partly this was due to the fact that Egyptian and Syrian monasticism was eremitic in orientation, which led to isolation and the tendency to be focused on one's own achievements. Moreover, while Mark 1:12–13 was the key text that inspired the Egyptian and Syrian ascetics to go out into the desert to fight demonic powers through fasting and other feats of asceticism, it was Acts 2:44 and 4:32—texts focused on community—that were the impetus behind Basilian monasticism.[15] Thus, Basil asks in his *Long Rules* 7, in which he is making the case for coenobitic monasticism:

> How will he show his humility, if there is no one with whom he may compare and so confirm his own greater humility? How will he give evidence of his compassion, if he has cut himself off from association with other

---

[14]Rousseau, *Basil of Caesarea*, 62.
[15]*Long Rules* 7, in Wagner, *Ascetical Works*, 252. See also Meredith, *Cappadocians*, 25.

persons? And how will he exercise himself in long-suffering, if no one contradicts his wishes?[16]

It also needs to be noted that Basil never really enjoyed robust health.[17] He had a severe liver complaint and frequently mentions it and other physical problems in his letters. In 368 he mentioned in passing in a letter to Eusebius of Samosata (d. 380), one of his closest friends, that his strength had been depleted by an illness that had kept him in bed for most of the previous winter.[18] Three years later he wrote of continual illnesses and being confined to his bed, expecting the end of his life at any moment.[19] In another letter to Eusebius, written in July or August of 373, Basil told him, "My body has failed me so completely that I cannot endure even the slightest movements without pain."[20] Another letter that year mentions his "liver complaint" and having had a fever for fifty days.[21] The following year he mentioned more fevers, diarrhea, and bowel problems.[22] In 375 or 376, writing to a physician named Meletius, he likened his weakened frame to "a spider's web."[23] Such physical problems were not conducive to a life of ascetic rigor.[24] It is extremely important to note that Basil could nevertheless say, "As long as we draw breath, we have the responsibility of leaving nothing undone for the edification of the churches of Christ."[25]

When Basil returned to Caesarea from his trip to Egypt and Syria in either 357 or 358, he joined his family's semimonastic household at Annesi in Pontus. Basil loved the natural beauty of the landscape around his ancestral home.[26] It was a household in which, according to Gregory of Nyssa, two things were

---

[16]*Long Rules* 7, in Wagner, *Ascetical Works*, 251, altered.

[17]See his *Letter* 203.

[18]*Letter* 27.

[19]*Letter* 30.

[20]*Letter* 100, in *Saint Basil: Letters*, trans. Agnes Clare Way, vol. 1 (New York: Fathers of the Church, 1951), 223.

[21]*Letter* 138, in Way, *Saint Basil: Letters*, 1:281.

[22]*Letter* 162, in Way, *Saint Basil: Letters*, 1:322.

[23]*Letter* 193, in *Saint Basil: Letters*, trans. Agnes Clare Way, vol. 2 (New York: Fathers of the Church, 1955), 39.

[24]Yet another reason why Basil was not prepared to implement the sort of monasticism found in Egypt and Syria was the climate of Asia Minor, which was very different from that of Egypt. Asia Minor had a cold climate in winter, which would have been injurious to the health of monks trying to live as if they were in the Egyptian desert. It was essential that Basil's monks not go far from the cities since they had more basic needs.

[25]*Letter* 203, in Way, *Saint Basil: Letters*, 2:69.

[26]Owen Chadwick, "Great Pastors—I. St. Basil the Great," *Theology* 56, no. 391 (1953): 21.

prominent: "constant prayer and the unceasing singing of hymns."[27] Over the next few years he was intermittently joined in this practice of the ascetic life by his friend Nazianzen. The two began work on the *Philocalia*, a compilation of texts from Origen, whom Basil regarded as a theological mentor, though he was never uncritical of the third-century exegete. They also had time to read and meditate on the Scriptures and pray together.[28]

During the 360s Basil founded or reformed a number of monasteries. His *Longer Rules* and *Shorter Rules* were written for the regulation of life in these communities. What is critical to note is that Basil viewed these rules as expressing spiritual advice that was in keeping with the Scriptures. For Basil, "Scripture alone represented the true rule or law for life."[29] It also needs to be noted that Basilian monasticism formed the inspiration for Benedictine monasticism, the dominant form in western Europe between 500 and 1000. Benedict (ca. 480–ca. 550), the so-called father of western monasticism, explicitly urged his monks to read "the rule of our holy Father Basil."[30]

It was in the formation of these monastic communities and his appointment as bishop of Caesarea in 370 that Basil learned firsthand the realities of leadership. As a person Basil was shy and reserved—his brother spoke of "his silence [being] more effective than speech."[31] But he was not the last shy individual—one thinks of John Calvin—to be called into a position of prominence. Basil also learned in his monastic experience the need for the Christian leader to be a spiritual director. Early in his monastic career he sought out Eustathius of Sebaste as a spiritual guide. Eusebius of Samosata was also an important mentor and model for Basil's life. In turn, Basil was a mentor to Eusebius's nephew Antiochus and to Gregory of Nazianzus's cousin, Amphilochius of Iconium (ca. 340–ca. 395).

Striving for Humility

A key area in Basil's thinking about monastic and episcopal leadership was the responsibility of the monastic leader and bishop to be a man marked by humility. For pagan classical Greek authors "humility" (*tapeinophrosynē*) and its cognates were totally negative terms and derogatory in meaning.

---

[27] Gregory of Nyssa, *Life of Saint Macrina*, 30.

[28] *Letter 2*, which was written during this period of time, provides an excellent entry-point into Basil's thinking about the ascetic life not long after his conversion.

[29] Andrea Sterk, *Renouncing the World yet Leading the Church: The Monk-Bishop in Late Antiquity* (Cambridge, MA: Harvard University Press, 2004), 49.

[30] Cited by Meredith, *Cappadocians*, 24.

[31] Cited by Chadwick, "St. Basil the Great," 21, 23.

They regarded humility as the mark of a social inferior, and it was often associated with such adjectives as *ignoble, servile, abject, downcast,* and *slavish.* A. L. Rowse, an English historian of the twentieth century, well capsulizes this pagan view of humility when he states in his autobiography of his early years, *A Cornish Childhood,* "I never for a moment understood why humility should be regarded as a virtue: I thought it contemptible."[32]

It is not at all surprising that the anthropocentric worldview of the pagan Greek authors would regard humility as shameful. In their eyes, there was nothing exalted about the position of a social inferior, for example, that of a slave. By contrast, the theocentric worldview of the New Testament saw in humility one of the best ways to describe man's relationship to God. In the mind of the New Testament authors, humility teaches us how lowly men and women really are before God.

Ultimately, it was the fragrant humility of Christ's life—from his humble birth through his life of selfless service, to his humiliating death on the cross— that transformed the meaning of this word. He was humility itself. As he said in Matthew 11:28–29: "Come to me, all you who labor and are heavy laden, and I will give you rest. Take my yoke upon you, and learn from me, for I am gentle and lowly [*tapeinos*] in heart, and you will find rest for your souls." Christ here describes himself as the ultimate embodiment of humility. Henceforth, all who genuinely called him Lord would seek to reproduce in their lives their Master's humility. And when the early Christians reflected on the meaning of Christ's coming into this world, his humility was central to their reflections. A good example of such reflection is Basil's *Homily* 20, *Of Humility.*[33] Like many of his sermons, it cannot be dated more precisely than saying it was given between 363 and 378.

Basil begins by explaining just how necessary it is for men and women to strive to be humble:

> Would that man had abided in the glory which he possessed with God—he would have genuine instead of fictitious dignity. For he would be ennobled by the power of God, illumined with divine wisdom, and made joyful in the possession of eternal life and its blessings. But, because he ceased to desire divine glory in expectation of a better prize, and strove for the unattainable, he lost the good which it was in his power to possess. The surest salvation for him, the remedy of his ills, and the means of restoration to his original

---

[32] *A Cornish Childhood* (1942; repr., London: Jonathan Cape, 1974), 155.
[33] Wagner, *Ascetical Works,* 475–86.

state is in practicing humility and not pretending that he may lay claim to any glory through his own efforts but seeking it from God.[34]

The way of salvation—Basil assures his hearers then, and his readers now—is a path of humility. Lest one think that Basil is here asserting some kind of works-righteousness, look at the final sentence. There Basil emphasizes that possessing the hope of eternal glory is the gift of God, given only to those who humble themselves to accept it. It cannot be achieved by human effort. As Basil states elsewhere, escape from "the condemnation due our sins" can happen only "if we believe in the grace of God [given] through his only-begotten Son."[35]

The sermon's focus, in a sense, is the acquisition of glory—the glory lost by Adam in the garden, that glory by which a man is "ennobled by the power of God, illumined with divine wisdom, and made joyful in the possession of eternal life and its blessings." It cannot be found through wealth or political power—which brings with it "a glory more unsubstantial than a dream"—nor "strength of arm, swiftness of foot, and comeliness of body" or human wisdom.[36] What is true glory then? Simply this: knowing the living God.

> But what is true glory and what makes a man great? "In this," says the Prophet, "let him that glories, glory that he understands and knows that I am the Lord" [Jer. 9:24]. This constitutes the highest dignity of man, this is his glory and greatness: truly to know what is great and to cleave to it, and to seek after glory from the Lord of glory. The Apostle tells us: "He that glories may glory in the Lord," saying: "Christ was made for us wisdom of God, righteousness and sanctification and redemption; that, as it is written: he that glories may glory in the Lord" [1 Cor. 1:30–31]. Now, this is the perfect and consummate glory in God: not to exult in one's own righteousness, but, recognizing oneself as lacking true righteousness, to be justified by faith in Christ alone.[37]

Foundational to humility, Basil argues here, is the recognition by men and women that they are entirely destitute of all true righteousness and holiness. To obtain these one must cast oneself upon God's mercy and

---

[34]*Homily* 20.1, in Wagner, *Ascetical Works*, 475.
[35]*Concerning Baptism* 1.2 (my translation).
[36]*Homily* 20.1–2, in Wagner, *Ascetical Works*, 475–78, passim.
[37]*Homily* 20.3, in Wagner, *Ascetical Works*, 478–79, altered.

so confess that one is made right with God—i.e., justified—by Christ alone.[38] In other words, becoming a Christian is intrinsically a humbling experience. What makes human beings truly great—what brings them glory, something that the ancients passionately sought—is to look away from themselves to God.

This passage clearly reveals Basil's fundamental opposition to any idea that we can save ourselves by our own good works, the very idea enunciated within thirty years of Basil's death by the heretic Pelagius (fl. 400–420). In other words, Basil's thought here is a foreshadowing of the developed thinking of Augustine, who, in responding to Pelagius, argued for the utter freeness of God's mercy and grace and that sinners cannot ultimately merit these gifts of God.[39] Basil, in fact, cites in his sermon 1 Corinthians 4:7, which was Augustine's favorite verse in this regard: "For what do you have that you have not received? And if you have received it, why do you glory as if you had not received it?"[40] Little wonder that when the sixteenth-century Reformers sought to argue that their view of saving grace was not so novel as their Roman Catholic opponents maintained, this Basilian text was one to which they turned.[41]

Humility thus leads the believer to recognize that he or she has nothing at all about which to boast. Our knowledge of God, our good deeds, and our possessions are all entirely rooted in the grace, goodness, and mercy of God. Basil elaborates:

> Why . . . do you glory in your goods as if they were your own instead of giving thanks to the Giver for His gifts? "For what do you have that you have not received? And if you received, why do you glory as if you had not received it?" [1 Cor. 4:7]. You have not known God by reason of your righteousness, but God has known you by reason of his goodness. "After that you have known God," says the Apostle, "or rather are known by God." You did not apprehend Christ because of your virtue, but Christ apprehended you by his coming.[42]

---

[38] David Amand, *L'Ascèse monastique de saint Basile* (Maredsous, France: Editions Maredsous, 1948), 313.

[39] Ibid., 313n230.

[40] *Homily* 20.4, in Wagner, *Ascetical Works*, 480, altered.

[41] See D. F. Wright, "Basil the Great in the Protestant Reformers," *Studia Patristica*, ed. Elizabeth A. Livingston (Oxford: Pergamon, 1982), 17/3:1153.

[42] *Homily* 20.4, in Wagner, *Ascetical Works*, 480, altered.

Basil therefore urges all of his hearers, both past and present, to "strive for glory with God, for his is a glorious reward."[43] This striving for glory with God is, in Basil's perspective, *the* most important practical demonstration of humility.

But what practical steps can a person make to grow in the grace of humility, all the while remembering that, for Basil, humility is fundamentally a work of the Holy Spirit? Because the Lord Jesus is the living paradigm of what humility looks like, constant reflection and meditation on his life are essential for growth in humility.

> In everything which concerns the Lord we find lessons in humility. As an infant, he was straightway laid in a cave, and not upon a couch but in a manger. In the house of a carpenter and of a mother who was poor, he was subject to his mother and her spouse. He was taught and he paid heed to what he needed not to be told. He asked questions, but even in the asking he won admiration for his wisdom. He submitted to John—the Lord received baptism at the hands of his servant. He did not make use of the marvellous power that he possessed to resist any of those who attacked him, but, as if yielding to superior force, he allowed temporal authority to exercise the power proper to it. He was brought before the high priest as though a criminal and then led to the governor. He bore calumnies in silence and submitted to his sentence, although he could have refuted the false witnesses. He was spat upon by slaves and by the vilest menials. He delivered himself up to death, the most shameful death known to men. Thus, from his birth to the end of his life, he experienced all the exigencies that befall mankind and, after displaying humility to such a degree, he manifested his glory, associating with himself in glory those who had shared his disgrace.[44]

Like the Puritans of a later day, Basil is not reticent to give specific advice to different groups of believers. For example, addressing wealthy Christians, Basil urges them to recognize the hand of God in all that they possess and not to glory in their riches as if they had acquired them without divine grace: Again:"Why, then, pray do you glory in your goods as if they were your own instead of giving thanks to the Giver for his gifts?'For what do you have that you have not received? And if you have received it, why do you glory as if you had not received it?'" (1 Cor. 4:7).[45] For Basil, humility is intimately bound

---

[43] *Homily* 20.7, in Wagner, *Ascetical Works*, 485, altered.
[44] *Homily* 20.6, in Wagner, *Ascetical Works*, 483–84, altered.
[45] *Homily* 20.4, in Wagner, *Ascetical Works*, 480, altered.

up with the awareness of the grace of God that pervades all of life and thus should lead the believer to a humble dependence upon God.

Basil was also not slow to reprove those who were prone to look down on others whose Christian maturity was questionable.

> That stern Pharisee, who, in his arrogant pride, not only boasted of himself but also discredited the publican in the presence of God, made his "righteousness" void by being guilty of pride. The publican went down justified in preference to him because he had given glory to God, the Holy One, and did not dare to lift his eyes, but sought only to win mercy, accusing himself by his posture, [and] by striking his breast. . . . Be on your guard, therefore, and bear in mind this example of grievous loss sustained through arrogance. . . . Never place yourself above anyone, not even great sinners.[46]

Basil urged attention to all of the details of life so as to root out pride from every crevice of our beings. Humility, in other words, must be a daily practice and endeavor.

> Your manner of speaking and singing, your conversation with your neighbour, also, should aim at modesty rather than pretentiousness. Do not strive, I beg you, for artificial embellishment in speech, for cloying sweetness in song, or for a . . . high-flown style in conversation. In all your actions, be free from pomposity. Be obliging to your friends, gentle toward your slaves, forbearing with the forward, benign to the lowly, a source of comfort to the afflicted, a friend to the distressed, a condemner of no one. . . . Speak not in your own praise, nor contrive that others do so.[47]

Humility is especially needful for those who are leaders. Basil urges them to be conscious of the fact that they are called to serve their brethren by their leadership, and not to lord it over them.[48]

> Suppose you have been deemed worthy of the episcopate and men throng about you and hold you in esteem. Come down to the level of your subordinates, "not as lording it over the clergy" [cf. 1 Pet. 5:3], and do not behave as worldly potentates do. The Lord bade him who wishes to be first to be the servant of all.[49]

---

[46] Homily 20.4, in Wagner, Ascetical Works, 481–82, altered.
[47] Homily 20.7, in Wagner, Ascetical Works, 484–85.
[48] Homily 20.7, in Wagner, Ascetical Works, 485–86.
[49] Homily 20.7, in Wagner, Ascetical Works, 485–86.

As Basil concludes the sermon, he comes back to the main theme announced at the beginning, namely, finding true glory.

> Strive for glory with God, for his is a glorious reward.... Strive after humility as becomes a lover of this virtue. Love it and it will glorify you. Then you will travel to good purpose the road leading to that true glory which is to be found with the angels and with God. Christ will acknowledge you as his own disciple before the angels and he will glorify you if you imitate his humility.[50]

At the heart of Basil's experience of the monastic life was a lifelong passion to be a holy man. He rightly understood that the Christian life is not simply an embrace of certain orthodox notions, just as the church catholic is far more than a coherent system of orthodox beliefs. For both the individual Christian and the church, it is a life of holiness lived in humility for the glory of God. True Christianity is both orthodoxy and "orthopraxy," and both of these, for Basil, are rooted in the life-giving work of the Holy Spirit. As such, it is not surprising that Basil also played a key role in the articulation of the orthodox doctrine of the Trinity. His chief theological work, *On the Holy Spirit*, written in 375, marked a decisive step toward the resolution of a controversy that had been raging among the churches since 318.

The Arian Controversy

At the beginning of the fourth century there had emerged a studied rejection of the full deity of the Son and the Spirit. Through the teaching of Arius (260/280–336), an elder and one-time popular preacher in the church at Alexandria, the church throughout the Roman Empire was plunged into a lengthy, bitter controversy about the person of Christ and his Spirit that dominated much of the fourth century.[51]

Arius's career before 318, when his views became controversial, is shadowy. It was in that year that he publicly claimed that only the Father was truly God.

---

[50] *Homily* 20.7, in Wagner, *Ascetical Works*, 485–86, altered.

[51] For studies of this controversy, see especially Jaroslav Pelikan, *The Christian Tradition: A History of the Development of Doctrine*, vol. 1, *The Emergence of the Catholic Tradition (100–600)* (Chicago: University of Chicago Press, 1971), 172–225; R. P. C. Hanson, *The Search for the Christian Doctrine of God: The Arian Controversy 318–381* (1988; repr., Grand Rapids: Baker, 2005); John Behr, *The Formation of Christian Theology*, vol. 2 in 2 parts, *The Nicene Faith* (Crestwood, NY: St Vladimir's Press, 2004). On Arius, see Behr, *The Nicene Faith*, part 1, 130–49. For a succinct statement of the philosophical and theological roots of Arianism, see Johannes Roldanus, *The Church in the Age of Constantine: The Theological Challenges* (Abingdon, UK: Routledge, 2006), 74–77.

As he wrote in a letter to Alexander (d. 328), the bishop of Alexandria, God the Father alone, "the cause of all, is without beginning." The Son was created by the Father as "an immutable and unchangeable perfect creature," and thus is "not everlasting or co-everlasting with the Father."[52] In Arius's words, "the Son has a beginning, but God is without beginning."[53] For Arius there was a time when the Son did not exist, a time when it was inappropriate to call God "Father." As for the Holy Spirit, by Arius's reckoning, he was even less divine than the Son, for he was the first of the creatures made by the Son.

Arius claimed to be following Scripture, and it is important to note that this is where the key battle had to be fought. He cited texts like John 14:28—"the Father is greater than I"—or Colossians 1:15—where Christ is called "the first-born of all creation"—to buttress his position. Arius was also deeply fearful of Sabellianism. In seeking to avoid that heresy, though, he fell into the equally pernicious error of denying the full deity of the Son and the Spirit.

Alexander's initial response was to emphasize that the Son is indeed as eternal as God the Father. According to Arius, Alexander taught, "Always God always Son," that is, the Son is coeternal with the Father.[54] Thus, there never was a time when the Father was without his Son. As such, the Son must be fully God.[55] Alexander summoned Arius to a meeting of all the church leaders of Alexandria and urged him to reconsider his views. When Arius refused, an open breach became unavoidable. In 321 Alexander convened a council of about one hundred elders from Egypt and Libya, which drew up a creed that repudiated Arius's novel views. When Arius and those who supported him refused to accept this document, the council had no choice but to excommunicate them. But Arius had no intention of letting things rest. He began to correspond with other church leaders outside of North Africa and thus took the definitive step that spread the conflict to the rest of the church in the Eastern Roman Empire.

What was especially difficult about this conflict was the "slippery" nature of Arius's views. For instance, he could call Jesus "God." But what he and his partisans understood by this term was very different from what Alexander and his friends meant by the term. For Arius, Jesus was "God" but not fully God like the Father. Arius did not consider him the eternal God, sharing in all the

---

[52]*Letter to Alexander of Alexandria*, in *The Trinitarian Controversy*, trans. William G. Rusch (Philadelphia: Fortress, 1980), 31–32.
[53]Arius, *Letter to Eusebius of Nicomedia*, in Rusch, *Trinitarian Controversy*, 29–30.
[54]Arius, *Letter to Eusebius of Nicomedia*, in Rusch, *Trinitarian Controversy*, 29–30.
[55]For a concise summary of Alexander's views, see Roldanus, *Church in the Age of Constantine*, 77.

attributes of the Father. In Arius's theology, the Son is really a creature, though the highest of all creatures.

Eventually, in the summer of 325, a council was called to provide definitive closure to the issue. Around 220 bishops and elders thus met at Nicaea, most of them from churches in the Eastern Roman Empire. The creedal statement that they issued, known to historians as the Nicene Creed, was designed to end the dispute with its unequivocal declaration that the Lord Jesus Christ is "true God of true God, begotten not made, of one being [homoousios] with the Father." In other words, the Son was confessed to be as truly God in whatever sense the Father is God. The key phrase in this creed is undoubtedly the statement that the Son is "of one being [homoousios] with the Father." Here, the full deity of the Son is asserted, the term homoousios emphasizing the fact that the Son shares the very being of the Father. Whatever belongs to and characterizes God the Father belongs to and characterizes the Son. He is not a creature, contrary to the view of Arius and his supporters.

It should be noted that the creed said nothing about the Spirit's divinity. This was because the heart of the controversy lay with regard to the nature of the Son. Nevertheless, something explicit in this regard needed to be confessed about the Spirit. But that confession as we shall see, would not come without further controversy.

In spite of what those who drafted this creed hoped, the Nicene Creed did not end the controversy. Eusebius of Nicomedia (d. ca. 342), a worldly wise ecclesiastical politician and supporter of Arius, had the ear of the professing Christian emperor, Constantine, who had played a central role in calling the ecumenical Council of Nicaea. When Constantine was convinced that the condemnation of Arianism was far too harsh, various Arian leaders and even Arius were brought back into favor from 327 onward, and the leading enthusiasts for Nicaea sent packing in the 330s.[56]

Controversy with Eustathius of Sebaste

Prominent in the defense of Nicene orthodoxy from the 330s to the 370s was Alexander of Alexandria's successor, Athanasius of Alexandria, a legend in his own time.[57] By the late 350s, Athanasius was compelled to advance his defense of the Nicene Creed and the deity of the Son to the question of the

---

[56]Ibid., 82–84.
[57]On the career and thought of Athanasius, see especially Alvyn Petersen, *Athanasius* (Ridgefield, CT: Morehouse, 1995); Khaled Anatolios, *Athanasius: The Coherence of His Thought* (New York: Routledge, 1998); Behr, *The Nicene Faith*, part 1, 163–259.

Spirit's full divinity.[58] And when Athanasius died in 373, Basil inherited his mantle.

In fact, at the time of Athanasius's death, Basil was locked in combat with professing Christians who, though they confessed the full deity of Christ, denied that the Spirit is fully God. Leading these "fighters against the Spirit" (Pneumatomachi), as they came to be called, was none other than the man who had been Basil's mentor, Eustathius of Sebaste. The controversy between Basil and Eustathius, from one perspective a part of the larger Arian controversy, has become known as the Pneumatomachian controversy.

Eustathius's interest in the Spirit seems to have been focused on the Spirit's work, not his person. For him, the Holy Spirit is primarily a divine gift within the Spirit-filled person, One who produces holiness.[59] When, on one occasion at a synod in 364, he was pressed to say what he thought of the Spirit's nature, he replied, "I neither chose to name the Holy Spirit God nor dare to call him a creature"![60]

For a number of years, Basil sought to win Eustathius over to the orthodox position. Finally, in the summer of 373 he met with him for an important two-day colloquy, in which, after much discussion and prayer, Eustathius finally acquiesced to an orthodox view of the Spirit's nature. At a second meeting Eustathius signed a statement of faith that said:

> [We] must anathematize those who call the Holy Spirit a creature, those who think so, and those who do not confess that he is holy by nature, as the Father and Son are holy by nature, but who regard him as alien to the divine and blessed nature. A proof of orthodox doctrine is the refusal to separate him from the Father and Son (for we must be baptized as we have received the words, and we must believe as we are baptized, and we must give honor as we have believed, to the Father, Son, and Holy Spirit), and to withdraw from the communion of those who call the Spirit a creature since they are clearly blasphemers. It is agreed (this comment is necessary because of the slanderers) that we do not say that the Holy Spirit is either unbegotten for

---

[58]See *The Letters of Saint Athanasius Concerning the Holy Spirit*, trans. C. R. B. Shapland (London: Epworth, 1951); and Michael A. G. Haykin, *The Spirit of God: The Exegesis of 1 and 2 Corinthians in the Pneumatomachian Controversy of the Fourth Century* (Leiden: E. J. Brill, 1994), 18–24, 59–103.

[59]Wolf-Dieter Hauschild, "Eustathius von Sebaste," *Theologische Realenzyklopädie* 10 (1982): 548–49. On Eustathius and his theological position, see also Haykin, *Spirit of God*, 24–49. On Eustathius's career, see also Jean Gribomont, "Eustathe de Sébaste," in *Dictionnaire de Spiritualité*, 4/2 (1961), 1708–12; C. A. Frazee, "Anatolian Asceticism in the Fourth Century: Eustathios of Sebastea and Basil of Caesarea," *The Catholic Historical Review* 66 (1980): 16–33.

[60]Socrates, *Church History* 2.45.

we know one unbegotten and one source of what exists, the Father of our Lord Jesus Christ, or begotten, for we have been taught by the tradition of the faith that there is one Only-Begotten. But since we have been taught that the Spirit of truth proceeds from the Father, we confess that he is from God without being created.[61]

In Basil's thinking, since the Spirit is holy without qualification, he cannot be a creature and must be indivisibly one with the divine nature. The confession of this unity is both the criterion of orthodoxy and the basis upon which communion can be terminated with those who assert that the Spirit is a creature. This pneumatological position thus defines the precise limits beyond which Basil was not prepared to venture, even for a friend such as Eustathius.

Yet another meeting was arranged for the autumn of 373, at which Eustathius would sign this declaration in the presence of a number of Christian leaders. But on the way home from his meeting with Basil, Eustathius was convinced by some of his friends who had been at the meeting that Basil was deeply in error. For the next two years Eustathius crisscrossed what is now modern Turkey denouncing Basil and claiming that the bishop of Caesarea was a Sabellian or modalist, that is, one who believed that there are absolutely no distinctions between the persons of the Godhead.

Basil was so stunned by what had transpired that he kept his peace for close to two years. As he wrote later, in 376, he was "astounded at so unexpected and sudden a change" in Eustathius that he was unable to respond. And, he went on to say:

> For my heart was crushed, my tongue was paralyzed, my hand benumbed, and I experienced the suffering of an ignoble soul . . . and I almost fell into misanthropy. . . . [So] I was not silent through disdain . . . but through dismay and perplexity and the inability to say anything proportionate to my grief.[62]

On the Holy Spirit

Finally, though, Basil simply felt that he had to speak. His words formed one of the most important books of the entire Patristic period, *On the Holy Spirit*, published in 375.[63] The immediate occasion of the treatise was a question

---

[61]Basil, *Letter* 125.3 (my translation).
[62]Basil, *Letter* 244.4 (my translation).
[63]For further reading on the Pneumatomachian controversy and Basil's role in it, see Haykin, *The Spirit of God*, 24–49, 104–69; Howard Griffith, "The Churchly Theology of Basil's *De Spiritu Sancto*," *Presbyterion*:

from Amphilochius of Iconium about what was the correct form of doxological address to God. The Pneumatomachi maintained it had to be something like, "We give glory to the Father *through* the Son *in* the Holy Spirit." Their refusal to confess that the Holy Spirit is fully divine clearly shaped their argument in this regard. Basil, on the other hand, was committed to the complete deity of the Spirit, and thus could offer "glory to the Father with the Son, together with the Holy Spirit."[64] After showing why Christians believe in the deity of Christ (chaps. 1–8), Basil devotes the heart of his treatise to demonstrating from Scripture why the Spirit is to be *equally* glorified together with the Father and the Son (chaps. 9–27) and thus implicitly recognized as God. The baptismal formula of Matthew 28:19 is absolutely central to his argument, for it reveals that the Spirit is inseparable from the divine being of the Father and the Son. The baptismal formula to be used in the rite of baptism does not run this way: "in the names of the Father and the Son and the Holy Spirit." Mention is made only of the singular *name* of the three, which is a distinct indication of their unity. There is only one God who has revealed himself as "the Father and the Son and the Holy Spirit."[65] Moreover, as the church baptizes, so must she teach and so must she worship. If she baptizes in the name of the Father and of the Son and of the Holy Spirit, she must teach the deity of the three and the propriety of their worship.

Moreover, ranked alongside, not below, the Father and the Son, the Spirit participates with the Father and the Son in the entirety of divine activity, from the creation of the angelic beings to the last judgment. For instance, the Spirit gives insight into divine mysteries, since he plumbs the depths of God (1 Cor. 2:10), something that only one who is fully divine can do.[66] He enables men and women to confess the true identity of Christ and worship him (1 Cor. 12:3).[67] These two texts clarified for Basil how salvation is imparted: through the power of the Spirit men and women come to a saving knowledge about God's redemptive work in the crucified Christ and are enabled to call him Lord. If the Spirit, therefore, is not fully divine, the work of salvation is short-circuited, for creatures simply cannot give such saving knowledge. Moreover,

Covenant Seminary Review 25 (1999): 91–108; and Mark J. Larson, "A Re-examination of *De Spiritu Sancto*: Saint Basil's Bold Defence of the Spirit's Deity," *Scottish Bulletin of Evangelical Theology* 19, no. 1 (Spring 2001): 65–84; Hildebrand, *Trinitarian Theology of Basil of Caesarea.*
[64]Basil, *On the Holy Spirit* 1.3.
[65]Basil, *On the Holy Spirit* 10.24; 10.26; 12.28; 13.30; 17.43; 18.44.
[66]Basil, *On the Holy Spirit* 16.40; 24.56.
[67]Basil, *On the Holy Spirit* 18.47.

the Spirit is omnipresent (Ps. 139:7), an attribute possessed only by God.[68] And he is implicitly called "God" by Peter (Acts 5:3–4).[69]

The Source of Holiness

Introducing Basil's entire argument is chapter 9, which breathes a different tone than does the main section of the book. It may well have been a meditation on the Spirit that Basil gave on a separate occasion, possibly to a monastic audience, and that Basil felt was a perfect introduction to the main section of the work because of its nonpolemical nature.[70]

> [The Holy Spirit] lives not because he is endowed with life, but because he is the giver of life, . . . the source of sanctification. . . . Now the relationship existing between the Spirit and our souls is not one of local proximity, for how can you bodily-wise draw near to the incorporeal? But it consists in the forsaking of lusts which, fostered by the love of the flesh, fasten on the soul and alienate it from its fellowship with God. Hence it is only by being purified from shame, the stain incurred through wickedness, and by returning to our natural beauty, and as it were by cleansing and restoring the King's image, that we can approach the Paraclete. And he, like the sun, when your sight is purged, will show you in himself the image of the invisible. And in the blessed vision of the image you shall see the ineffable beauty of the archetype. Through him hearts are lifted up, the weak are taken by the hand, those advancing are perfected. He, shedding his bright beams upon those who are cleansed from every stain, makes them spiritual by their communion with himself. And as clear, transparent bodies, if a ray of light fall upon them, become radiant themselves and diffuse their splendour all around, so souls illuminated by the indwelling Spirit are rendered spiritual themselves, and impart their grace to others. Thence comes the knowledge of the future, the understanding of mysteries, the comprehension of secrets, the distribution of gifts, the heavenly life, companionship with angels, unending joy, abiding in God, likeness to God, the utmost of our heart's desires,—the being God. Such, in brief, are the views which we have been taught by the oracles of the Spirit themselves to hold respecting the greatness, the dignity, and the operations of the Holy Spirit.[71]

---

[68]Basil, *On the Holy Spirit* 23.54.

[69]Basil, *On the Holy Spirit* 16.37.

[70]Here I follow Hermann Dörries's superb monograph *De Spiritu Sancto: Der Beitrag des Bailius zum Abschluss des trinitarischen Dogmas* (Göttingen: Vandenhoeck & Ruprecht, 1956), 54–56.

[71]*On the Holy Spirit* 9.22–23, in *Basil the Great . . . On the Holy Spirit*, rev. ed., trans. George Lewis, Christian Classics Series 4 (London: Religious Tract Society, nd), 53–54.

While Basil is quick to affirm throughout this treatise as a whole that the source of our holiness is the Spirit, this passage does introduce a contrary notion: to come to the Spirit for sanctification we must have purified our souls. At a later point in this treatise, though, the Cappadocian divine can affirm that the Lord Jesus bestows on his disciples the desire to welcome the grace of the Spirit.[72] One finds a similar ambiguity in Basil's brother, Gregory of Nyssa. For example, in Gregory's account of the death of his and Basil's sister in his *Life of Saint Macrina*, Gregory highlights the role that Macrina's will played in her piety by totally controlling her emotions as she faced death. At the same time, Gregory clearly states at one point that his sister's godliness was a result of the "indwelling grace of the Holy Spirit."[73] The ambiguity of the Cappadocian theologians at this point is traceable in part to the fact that the primacy of divine grace had not yet become a major issue of contention, as it would at the beginning of the fifth century with the Pelagian controversy. In part, the stress on human freedom also goes back to the church's battle with Gnostic determinism in the second century.

What is most significant about the above passage, though, is Basil's emphasis that in the Spirit we see the Son, "the image of the invisible," and in the Son, we are led to the vision of "the ineffable beauty of the archetype," that is, the Father.[74] This way of ascent to the Father also informs Basil's understanding of worship. As he states later in *On the Holy Spirit*:

> In worship the Holy Spirit is inseparable from the Father and the Son. For dissociated from him you will not worship at all; but being in him you cannot by any means separate him from God, any more than you can sever the light from things seen, for it is impossible to see the image of God, except by the illumination of the Spirit. And he who gazes upon the image cannot sever the light from the image, for the cause of vision is of necessity seen together with the things we see. So then . . . through the illumination of the Spirit we behold the effulgence of the glory of God; and through the impress we are led up to him of whom he is the impress and exact representation.[75]

---

[72] *On the Holy Spirit* 22.53.

[73] Gregory of Nyssa, *The Life of Saint Macrina*, 36. See also David Roach, "Macarius the Augustinian: Grace and Salvation in the Spiritual Homilies of Macarius-Symeon," *Eusebeia: The Bulletin of the Andrew Fuller Center for Baptist Studies* 8 (Fall 2007): 91–92.

[74] For the same point, see Basil, *On the Holy Spirit* 18.47; 26.64; *Letter* 226.3.

[75] Basil, *On the Holy Spirit* 26.64, in Lewis, *Basil the Great . . . On the Holy Spirit*, 123.

In both of these passages from *On the Holy Spirit* Basil is building on such passages as Hebrews 1:3 and Colossians 1:15, in which the Son is described as the image of the Father, whom Basil calls the "Archetype." During the course of the Arian controversy, it had become a commonplace to argue that the Son's being the image of the Father meant that there was a community of nature between the Son and the Father. But knowledge of the image and by extension its Archetype is impossible without the Spirit, who reveals the Son—here Basil is drawing upon 1 Corinthians 12:3. Moreover, this knowledge is given by the Spirit "in himself." Knowledge and worship of God does not come through an intermediary like an angel, but is given by God by or in himself—namely, in the Spirit, who must therefore be divine. This text then tells us why the Spirit is inextricably joined to the Father and the Son. His epistemic and doxological relationship to the Father and the Son speaks of an ontological union.[76] As Basil noted in one of his letters, "Therefore we never divorce the Paraclete from his unity with the Father and the Son; for our mind when it is lit by the Spirit looks up to the Son and in him as in an image beholds the Father."[77]

Now, if the Spirit is God, how does his relationship to the Father differ from that of the Son to the Father? This was a vital question for fourth-century Greek theologians since they ever feared the specter of Sabellianism, which denied the hypostatic differences between the persons within the Godhead. Basil turned to such Scripture texts as John 15:26, 1 Corinthians 2:12, and Psalm 33:6 to argue that the Spirit "proceeds from the mouth of the Father and is not begotten like the Son."[78] Basil quickly qualified this image. The terms *breath* and *mouth* must be understood in a manner befitting to God. The comparison of the Spirit with breath does not mean that he is the same as human breath, which quickly dissipates upon exhalation, for the Spirit is a living being with the power to sanctify others. This image well reflects the nature of our knowledge about God. On the one hand, it indicates the intimate relationship of the Father and the Spirit, so the Spirit has to be glorified with the Father and the Son. On the other hand, the image reminds us that the Spirit's mode of existence is ineffable, even as the being of the Godhead is beyond human comprehension.[79]

---

[76]Hildebrand, *Trinitarian Theology of Basil of Caesarea*, 187, 190–91.
[77]Basil, *Letter* 226.3 (my translation).
[78]*On the Holy Spirit* 18.46; see also 16.38.
[79]Haykin, *Spirit of God*, 143–47.

Moreover, Basil affirms in the passage from *On the Holy Spirit* 9 cited above, such communion with God has a deeply transformative effect upon those privileged to participate in it. The Holy Spirit makes them "spiritual," vehicles of spiritual grace to other human beings, even as a transparent substance, when sunlight falls upon it, sheds radiance around itself.[80] The spiritual radiance of such believers never ceases to be a gift, but it is nevertheless a true radiance from the Spirit of God. And surely this is what Basil means when he says that the ultimate result of this communion through and with the Spirit results in "the utmost of our heart's desires,—the being God." This does not mean that believers ever cease to be finite creatures and actually become the Creator, certainly not in this world or the next. Rather, they so share in the communicable attributes of God that ultimately they become flawlessly loving, spotlessly holy, and so on.

It is all too easy for evangelical believers who are rightly taken up with exalting the grace of God to forget that such grace, when truly experienced, has a profound impact on a person's life. Basil's emphasis here surely has much to teach contemporary evangelicalism. Some reading Basil's words may well balk at the boldness of his claims. But it is fascinating to note that Jonathan Edwards, a paragon of evangelical piety, can make almost the identical observation in his spiritual masterpiece, *The Religious Affections*.

> The Spirit of God is given to the true saints to dwell in them, as his proper lasting abode.... And he is represented as being there so united to the faculties of the soul, that he becomes there a principle or spring of new nature and life. ... The light of the Sun of Righteousness do[es]n't only shine upon them, but is so communicated to them, that they shine also, and become little images of that Sun which shines upon them.[81]

The Triumph of Basil's Doctrine of the Spirit

Basil died on January 1, 379, worn out by hard work and illness, the latter probably associated with his liver. He never witnessed the triumph of the Trinitarianism for which he had fought for most of the 370s, though, as Rowan Greer puts it, "one hopes that like Moses he saw the promised land from afar."[82] His final recorded statement on the question of the Trinity was

---

[80]For the same point, see also Basil, *On the Holy Spirit* 21.52.

[81]*The Religious Affections*, ed. John E. Smith, The Works of Jonathan Edwards 2 (New Haven, CT: Yale University Press, 1959), 200–201.

[82]*Broken Lights and Mended Lives: Theology and Common Life in the Early Church* (University Park: Pennsylvania State University Press, 1986), 46.

given in a letter written in 376 or 377 to Epiphanius of Salamis (ca. 315–403). The latter had asked Basil to intervene in a doctrinal dissension over the question of the Spirit at a monastic community on the Mount of Olives. With regard to Epiphanius's request, Basil replied: "We are unable to add anything to the Nicene creed, not even the smallest addition, except the glorification of the Holy Spirit, because our fathers made mention of this part [of the faith] cursorily, since at that time no controversial question concerning it had yet arisen."[83] This passage is important for a couple of reasons. First, it provides, in summary form, the position that was reached in On the Holy Spirit: the Spirit is to be glorified together with the Father and the Son. Second, Basil thinks that this explanation entails an expansion of the third article of the Nicene Creed. That expansion came in the creed issued by a second ecumenical council called by the emperor Theodosius I (347–395).

With the death of the Emperor Valens (328–378), a protector of the Arians, in the disastrous battle against the Goths and Huns at Adrianople in Thrace (378), the purple passed to a Spaniard, Theodosius I, who, in his theological convictions, was committed to Nicene Trinitarianism. Determined to establish the church on the bedrock of the Nicene Creed, Theodosius traveled to Constantinople, entering the city on November 24, 380, whereupon he called a council to meet in Constantinople the following May.

Theodosius desired the Nicene theologians at the council to see if they could persuade the Pneumatomachi to abandon their deficient view of the Spirit. However, the gulf that lay between the orthodox and the Pneumatomachi, thirty-six bishops under the leadership of Eleusius of Cyzicus—Eustathius appears to have been dead—was so wide that it could not have been bridged without one side sacrificing all that they held dear. Thus, the Pneumatomachi, after rejecting the proposed union, left the council. After their departure, the council approved a confessional statement that may well have been crafted in the discussions with the Pneumatomachi, as Adolf-Martin Ritter has argued.[84] Moreover, it is quite probable that one of the leading figures behind the composition of this creedal statement was Basil's younger brother, Nyssen. Gregory had drunk deeply from the well of both Scripture and his brother's doctrine of the Spirit.

Without a doubt, the Niceno-Constantinopolitan Creed is one of the most significant texts from the early church. The third article, which deals

---

[83]Basil, Letter 258.2.
[84]Das Konzil von Konstantinopel und sein Symbol: Studien zur Geschichte und Theologie des II. Ökumenischen Konzils (Göttingen: Vandenhoeck & Ruprecht, 1965).

with the Holy Spirit, runs thus: "We believe in the Holy Spirit, the Lord, the giver of life, who proceeds from the Father. With the Father and the Son he is worshipped and glorified. He has spoken through the Prophets." The opening description of the Holy Spirit as "Lord," which was drawn from 2 Corinthians 3:17, recalls a key part of Basil's argument for the deity of the Spirit.[85] Then, terming the Spirit as "the giver of life" is probably meant to highlight the Spirit's giving of not simply physical life, but also supernatural life in regeneration, sanctification, and glorification, which were all key concerns of Basil.

The clause "who proceeds from the Father" is taken from John 15:26. One significant change, though, was made: in place of the preposition "from the side of" (*para*) in John 15:26 there is the preposition "from within" (*ek*), a change based on 1 Corinthians 2:12. This clause serves to differentiate the person of the Spirit from the person of the Son. Whereas the Son is begotten of the Father, the Spirit proceeds from the Father. In the words of Harold O. J. Brown, "Ultimately this language tells us . . . that the Father, the Son, and the Holy Spirit are distinct Persons." It thus secures Basil's concern to avoid Sabellianism and affirms that "in the Trinity we are dealing with three distinctive Persons, not merely with modes or appearances of one and the same Person."[86] Note also that the verb "proceeds" is in the present tense, which is tantamount to saying that, like the Father and the Son, the Spirit had no beginning.[87]

The next clause—the "all-important clause" as J. N. D Kelly puts it—is "with the Father and the Son he is worshipped and glorified."[88] As it stands, it would have been impossible for the Pneumatomachi to have subscribed to this statement.[89] This statement is clearly indebted to the argument of Basil in his *On the Holy Spirit*, where he had shown from the Scriptures that the Spirit's co-adoration and conglorification with the Father and the Son is only right and proper.

The final clause, "who spoke through the prophets," is based on verses like 2 Peter 1:20–21 and Ephesians 3:5. While it may have primary reference to the Old Testament prophets,[90] it is important to note that Basil could

---

[85]See, for example, *On the Holy Spirit* 21.52.

[86]*Heresies* (Garden City, NY: Doubleday, 1984), 133.

[87]Ibid., 142–43.

[88]*Early Christian Creeds*, 2nd ed. (London: Longmans, Green and Co., 1960), 342.

[89]Ritter, *Konzil von Konstantinopel*, 301.

[90]A. de Halleux, "La Profession de l'Esprit-Saint dans le symbole de Constantinople," *Revue Théologique de Louvain* 10 (1979): 30.

describe the inspiration of the whole Bible as prophetic.[91] Undoubtedly he considered the prophetism of the Scriptures a proof of the divinity of the Spirit who inspired them.[92]

This article of the creed, like the rest of the creedal statement, must be viewed as a *norma normata*, "a rule that is ruled," not a *norma normans*, "a rule that rules," as Roman Catholic and Orthodox theologians assert when they postulate that this creed, along with other ancient creeds, is of absolute authority and infallible. Creeds are not infallible. Like other human formulations the creeds are subordinate to Scripture, the supreme rule of faith and practice. As Bruce Demarest once put it, the creeds "are worthy of honour to the degree that they accord with the teachings of the Word of God."[93] On the other hand, this pneumatological statement we have been considering, like the rest of the creed, is a rule that faithfully reflects the view of God in the Scriptures. And as such, it stands as one of the great landmarks of Christian theology, a fact that can never be taken lightly.[94] Neither Basil nor any of the other church fathers believed that a creedal statement like this captured the essence of the triune God. Rather, they spoke as they did because they could not remain silent, either in the face of heresy's onslaught or under the impact of their hearts' need to worship.

---

[91] Hildebrand, *Trinitarian Theology of Basil of Caesarea*, 109–14.
[92] De Halleux, "Profession de l'Esprit-Saint," 31.
[93] "The Contemporary Relevance of Christendom's Creeds," *Themelios* 7, no. 2 (January 1982): 15–16.
[94] Ibid., 15.

Chapter 7

SAVING THE IRISH

The Mission of Patrick

*This gospel of the kingdom will be proclaimed throughout the whole world
as a testimony to all nations, and then the end will come.*

MATTHEW 24:14

Scholars have long reflected on and debated the reasons behind the fall of
the Western Roman Empire. A multitude of suggestions, ranging from
the ridiculous to the extremely plausible—things like climatic change,
lead poisoning of the aristocracy, excessive government bureaucracy, and the
demise of the urban middle class—have been made.[1] One classical approach,
that of the eighteenth-century historian Edward Gibbon (1737–1794), maintained that the fall was intimately tied to the growth of Christianity.[2] There
is no doubt that many of the most brilliant thinkers of late antiquity—some

---

An earlier version of this chapter appeared as "'Bound by the Spirit': An Appreciation of Patrick," in
For a Testimony [Mark 13:9]: Essays in Honour of John H. Wilson, ed. Michael A. G. Haykin (Toronto:
Central Baptist Seminary and Bible College, 1989), 45–61.

[1] See Donald Kagan, Steven Ozment, and Frank M. Turner, *The Western Heritage*, 6th ed. (Upper Saddle
River, NJ: Prentice Hall, 1998), 192–93. See the list of 210 suggestions—in German—for the fall of
Rome in Bryan Ward-Perkins, *The Fall of Rome and the End of Civilization* (Oxford: Oxford University
Press, 2005), 32.

[2] *History of the Decline and Fall of the Roman Empire*, 3 vols. (1776–1781).

of whom we have met: Hilary of Poitiers, Basil of Caesarea, John Chrysostom (ca. 347–407), and Augustine of Hippo—devoted their energies to the life of the church and not to that of the state and thereby possibly drained off valuable resources from the political sphere. But Gibbon's explanation is probably shaped as much by his bitter dislike of the Christian faith as by the historical evidence. Another perspective worth noting is that of Arther Ferrill, who has presented a convincing argument for a military explanation for the collapse of Roman hegemony in western Europe.[3] It is vital to note, however, that none of these various theories can be regarded as cogent if it does not account for why the West was submerged beneath a tidal wave of Germanic tribes while the eastern half of the empire continued in transmogrified form as the Byzantine Empire.[4]

Increasingly, however, historians of this period are reticent to talk of a "fall" of Roman imperial power. They much prefer to speak in terms of a "transformation," a transition from the empire of late antiquity to the various quasi-Romanized Germanic kingdoms of the early mediaeval era.[5] This perspective has a long pedigree, dating back at least to the time of Gibbon, when the Italian Abbé Ferdinand Galliani (1728–1787), the Neapolitan ambassador to France, wrote: "The fall of empires? What can that mean? Empires being neither up or down they do not fall. They change their appearance."[6] In recent days, the leading advocate of this position has been Peter Brown. In a reflective essay on *The World of Late Antiquity*, his 1971 book that argued for this new view of the closing days of the Roman world, Brown wrote that in this book he was able to discuss the history of this period without invoking "the widespread notion of decay."[7]

Nevertheless, as Bryan Ward-Perkins has argued in a recent study defending the traditional notion of a fall of Rome, if we look at the textual and material evidence from the period in question, we cannot escape the fact that "the coming of the Germanic peoples was very unpleasant for the Roman population, and . . . the long-term effects of the dissolution of the empire

---

[3] *The Fall of the Roman Empire: The Military Explanation* (London: Thames and Hudson, 1986). For an excellent overview of Roman military strategy and the military weaknesses that led to the collapse of Roman might, see Michael F. Pavkovic, "Grand Strategy of the Roman Empire," *Military Chronicles* 1, no. 1 (May/June 2005): 14–30.

[4] Barry Baldwin, "Roman Empire," in *Encyclopedia of Early Christianity*, ed. Everett Ferguson, 2nd ed. vol. 2 (New York: Garland, 1997), 993.

[5] John P. McKay, Bennett D. Hill, and John Buckler, *A History of Western Society*, 7th ed. (Boston: Houghton Mifflin, 2003), 184–85; Ward-Perkins, *Fall of Rome*, 3–5.

[6] Cited by McKay, Hill, and Buckler, *History of Western Society*, 184.

[7] "The World of Late Antiquity Revisited," *Symbolae Osloenses* 72 (1997): 14–15.

were dramatic."[8] And when one reads the various contemporary witnesses to this great historical event, it is invariably the notions of collapse, demise, and end that predominate. For instance, after the cataclysmic defeat of the Romans at the Battle of Adrianople in 378, when the emperor Valens, many of his senior officers, and close to two-thirds of the imperial army in the Eastern Roman Empire were slain by a combined army of Germanic Goths and the Huns, Ambrose, bishop of Milan and Augustine's early mentor, was certain that "the end of the world is coming" (*mundi finis*) and that he and his contemporaries were in "the wane of the age" (*occasu saeculi*).[9] Seventeen years later, the Bible scholar and translator Jerome, writing from the relative tranquility of a monastery in Bethlehem, was convinced after hearing of Hunnic invasions of the eastern empire that "the Roman world was falling" apart, and this had to mean the end of history.[10] And at the northernmost province of the Roman Empire, a young boy whom we know today as Patrick certainly experienced the traumatic passing of the empire as he was kidnapped and enslaved by Irish pirates.

Roman Rule in Britannia

When Patrick was born, the Romans had been in Britain for roughly 350 years. South of Hadrian's Wall they had crisscrossed the land with a network of Roman roads. Urban centers of importance, such as Eburacum (York), Glevum (Gloucester), and Londinium (London), had been developed, and dotting the countryside lavish villas had been built by the Romano-British upper class. Among these wealthy Britons there had grown to be an appreciation of and desire for Roman culture, and consequently they sought to ensure that their children received a proper Roman education. The historian Tacitus depicts this eagerness of the British upper classes to acquire Roman culture in a famous text from his biography of Agricola (40–93), the Roman general who was instrumental in extending Roman rule throughout Britain. Agricola "educated the sons of the [British] chiefs in the liberal arts," Tacitus informs us. And the "result was that instead of loathing the Latin language they became eager to speak it effectively. In the same way, our national dress came into favor and

---

[8]Ward-Perkins, *Fall of Rome*, 10.

[9]*Exposition of the Gospel according to Luke* 10.10. For a brief account of the events leading up to the battle and of the battle itself, see F. Homes Dudden, *The Life and Times of St. Ambrose*, vol. 1 (Oxford: Clarendon, 1935), 166–72.

[10]*Letter* 60.16, in *The Principal Works of St. Jerome*, trans. W. H. Freemantle, Nicene and Post-Nicene Fathers, Series 2, vol. 6 (repr., Grand Rapids: Eerdmans, 1978), 257, altered.

the toga was everywhere to be seen."[11] It is not surprising that the members of this social stratum became genuinely bilingual, conversant in both their native British and the Latin of their rulers. On the other hand, the lower classes, especially those in rural areas probably knew little, if any, Latin.[12] The ability of Patrick to write in Latin—albeit imperfectly, as we shall see—is a clue to his social origins: he was from the upper class of Romano-British society.[13]

At the close of the fourth century, however, the comfortable world of the Romanized British upper class was about to be shattered, never to be restored. During the last quarter of that century the empire had suffered a number of severe body blows that would precipitate the total collapse of imperial rule in the West in the following century. Those momentous events were naturally not without impact on Roman Britain.

During the winter of 406–407, the Rhine River, the natural northern frontier of the Western Roman Empire, froze to such an extent that a large number of Germanic warriors were able to cross over to ravage the Roman territories of Gaul and Hispania. They were never driven out. The following summer, Constantine III (d. 411), a usurper who had been elevated to imperial power by the legions in Britain, crossed the channel, ostensibly to repel the barbarians. The legions never returned.

In the decades that followed, the British sought to organize their own defense against Saxon raiders from the east and hit-and-run attacks by Irish pirates from the west. But with the departure of the legions, economic and cultural decay started to set in. Towns began to be deserted, and the lavish villas of the upper classes abandoned. The monetary system began to suffer decay, and the Roman system of education also probably collapsed.[14] But what did not collapse or leave with the Roman legions was the Christian witness on the island.

The British Church

While Patrick's writings constitute some of the earliest literary evidence from an actual member of the British church, there is written testimony going back

---

[11] *Agricola* 21, in *Tacitus: The Agricola and the Germania*, trans. H. Mattingly, rev. S. A. Handford (Harmondsworth, UK: Penguin, 1970), 72–73.

[12] Kenneth Jackson, *Language and History in Early Britain* (Edinburgh: Edinburgh University Press, 1953), 97–106.

[13] See the discussion of Patrick's social background by R. P. C. Hanson, *The Life and Writings of the Historical Saint Patrick* (New York: Seabury, 1983), 4–5; E. A. Thompson, *Who Was Saint Patrick?* (Woodbridge, UK: Boydell, 1985), 40–41; Máire B. de Paor, *Patrick: The Pilgrim Apostle of Ireland* (New York: HarperCollins, 1998), 26–28.

[14] Hanson, *Historical Saint Patrick*, 7.

to the second century regarding the presence of Christianity in the British Isles. In the 190s the North African author Tertullian, for instance, states in his *Adversus Judaeos* that Christianity had spread so far, it had reached Britain and had gone beyond the Antonine Wall. In answer to his question, "In whom else have all the nations believed, than in the Christ who has already come?" he states that even "places in Britain . . . , though inaccessible to the Romans, have yielded to Christ."[15] In the following century Origen, the learned Egyptian exegete, also shows an awareness that the Christian faith has secured adherents in Britain when he asks, "When ever did the land of Britain agree on the worship of one god before the arrival of Christ?" By the late second century or early third century, then, "British Christianity was sufficiently well-founded and its membership sufficiently large that Christians in North Africa and Alexandria" knew of its existence.[16]

How Christianity first came to the shores of Britain is impossible to determine. W. H. C. Frend has plausibly suggested that it was brought there by merchants or by soldiers garrisoned in Britain.[17] Be this as it may, it would not have taken root among the native Britons as it did if it had not been for persons like the second-century missionary-theologian Irenaeus, who learned Gaulish, the language of the Celts living in Gaul, in order to reach them with the gospel.[18] To reach the native Britons, there would have to have been some who, like Irenaeus, were willing to learn the "barbarous dialect" of the British natives. But very little is known, in the way of either literary or archaeological evidence, about the church in Britain up until the fourth century.

With the fourth century, however, a number of statements appear about the British church and its bishops from contemporary authors on the continent. One of some import is made by Athanasius of Alexandria to the effect that the British church had fully assented to the Nicene Creed and its condemnation of the fourth-century heresy Arianism.[19] As we shall see, a significant part of Patrick's spiritual bequest to the Celts in Ireland will be a doctrine of the Trinity that is in full accord with that of Nicaea.

---

[15] *Adversus Judaeos* 7. See also Joseph F. Kelly, "The Origins of Christianity in Britain: The Literary Evidence" (unpublished paper, May, 1983), 4–5.

[16] Kelly, "Origins of Christianity in Britain," 5. Cf. Henry Chadwick, *The Early Church*, rev. ed. (London: Penguin, 1993), 63, who believes that it was not until the middle of the third century that Christianity was securely established.

[17] "Romano-British Christianity and the West: Comparison and Contrast," in *The Early Church in Western Britain and Ireland*, ed. Susan M. Pearce (Oxford: B.A.R., 1982), 6.

[18] *Against Heresies* 1.Preface.3.

[19] *Letter to the Emperor Jovian* 2.

Archaeological evidence from third- and fourth-century Britain confirms a growing acceptance of Christianity by the upper classes, a movement that paralleled what was happening in the rest of the empire.[20] For example, archaeologists have uncovered Christian places of worship from the fourth and fifth centuries. The most interesting of these is perhaps at Lullingstone in Kent. There a villa has been unearthed that had been built toward the end of the first century and substantially expanded near the end of the following century by a person of some distinction and wealth. In the 360s and 370s, the owner of the villa became a Christian, and a small suite of rooms in one wing of the villa was specifically devoted to Christian usage and worship. After the withdrawal of the Roman legions in the early years of the fifth century, the villa was destroyed by fire and never rebuilt.[21] The remains of paintings on the walls of those rooms devoted to Christian usage contain distinctly Christian symbols. And on one of the walls there is a unique depiction of a series of figures, each about four feet tall, clothed in beautiful, brightly colored garments, standing in prayer. This was no doubt an estate chapel, available for the Christians who worked on the villa's property, as well as for the people who lived in the villa.[22]

By the turn of the fifth century we also encounter for the first time prominent British churchmen: men such as Pelagius (fl. 400), whose perspective on the Christian faith brought about a far-ranging controversy with that colossal thinker of antiquity Augustine, as well as with Faustus (ca. 408–ca. 490), bishop of Riez and a well-known preacher in Gaul,[23] and Ninian (fl. 400), a missionary working among the Picts in southwestern Scotland during the first half of the fifth century.[24]

---

[20]For a discussion of the evidence for the existence of Christianity in Britain up to and including the fourth century, see R. P. C. Hanson, *Saint Patrick: His Origins and Career* (Oxford: Clarendon, 1968), 30–34; Charles Thomas, *Christianity in Roman Britain to A.D. 500* (London: Batsford Academic and Educational, 1981); Kelly, "Origins of Christianity in Britain," 5–9; Philip Freeman, *St. Patrick of Ireland: A Biography* (New York: Simon & Schuster, 2004), 59–60.

[21]Roger J. A. Wilson, *A Guide to the Roman Remains in Britain* (London: Constable, 1975), 52–53.

[22]See H. H. Scullard, *Roman Britain: Outpost of the Empire* (London: Thames and Hudson, 1979), 119–21, 166–68; Hanson, *Historical Saint Patrick*, 8–9. Also see Chadwick, *Early Church*, 63:"A certainly Christian chapel in a wealthy villa of the fourth century has turned up at Lullingstone in Kent." The paintings, including the series of figures in worship, are now in the British Museum.

[23]For Faustus, see J. G. Cazenove,"Faustus (11)," *A Dictionary of Christian Biography*, ed. William Smith and Henry Wace, vol. 2 (London: John Murray, 1880), 467–70; Hanson, *Saint Patrick: His Origins and Career*, 63–65.

[24]The major source for the life and ministry of Ninian is Bede, *Church History* 3.4. For a discussion of this text from Bede and Ninian's ministry, see Hanson, *Saint Patrick: His Origins and Career*, 56–63; Thomas, *Christianity in Roman Britain*, 275–94.

The picture of the British church that emerges from this brief sketch is of a church that had made sufficient headway on the island to have a number of bishops. It was able to produce theologians and scholars of the caliber of Pelagius and Faustus. And it was seeking to evangelize, at least to some degree, through the likes of a Ninian.[25]

The Career of Patrick

Such is the context into which the life and career of Patrick must be placed if it is to be properly appreciated. Now, the dates of Patrick's birth and death have been, and still are, the subject of much debate. Hanson has put forward a fairly convincing argument in favor of placing Patrick's birth around 389 and his death some 70 years later, around 461, but he admits that these dates possess no finality.[26] What is certain is that Patrick is a product of Britain in the late fourth century, and his missionary activity in Ireland falls mostly within the first half of the fifth century.[27]

The broad outline of Patrick's career is fairly plain. At the beginning of his *Confession*, one of two texts that come from the hand of Patrick, he tells us of his family background and how his life at home was traumatically interrupted.

> I am Patrick, a sinner, most unlearned, the least of all the faithful, and utterly despised by many. My father was Calpornius, a deacon, son of Potitus, a presbyter, of the village Bannavem Taburniae; he had a country seat [*villulam*] nearby, and there I was taken captive. I was then about sixteen years of age. I did not know the true God. I was taken into captivity to Ireland with many thousands of people—and deservedly so, because we turned away from God, and did not keep his commandments, and did not obey our bishops, who used to remind us of our salvation. And the Lord "brought over us the wrath of his anger"[28] and "scattered us among many

---

[25] Hanson, *Saint Patrick: His Origins and Career*, 69–71; Thomas, *Christianity in Roman Britain*, 198; Freeman, *St. Patrick of Ireland*, xviii, 197.

[26] *Saint Patrick: His Origins and Career*, 171–88. See also Hanson and Cecile Blanc, *Saint Patrick: Confession et Lettre à Coroticus* (Paris: Les Éditions du Cerf, 1978), 18–21. For other perspectives on Patrick's dates, see Thomas, *Christianity in Roman Britain*, 314–46, passim; Thompson, *Who Was Saint Patrick?*, 166–75. For a strong argument in favor of a later dating, see David N. Dumville, *Saint Patrick, A.D. 493–1993* (Woodbridge, UK: Boydell, 1993), 29–33. John T. Koch has argued for a much earlier dating, ca. 351–ca. 428; see his "The Early Chronology for St Patrick (c. 351–c. 428): Some New Ideas and Possibilities," in *Celtic Hagiography and Saints' Cults*, ed. Jane Cartwright (Cardiff: University of Wales Press, 2003), 102–22.

[27] *Saint Patrick: His Origins and Career*, 187.

[28] Isa. 42:25.

nations,"[29] even "unto the utmost part of the earth"[30] where now my littleness is placed among strangers.[31]

Patrick was raised in what appears to have been a nominal Christian home. He states in this text that his father, Calpornius, was both a deacon and the owner of a villa. In the only other literary text to come from the hand of Patrick, his *Letter to the Soldiers of Coroticus*, we also learn that his father had a number of "men and women servants" and that Calpornius was also a decurion, that is, an official of the local town council.[32] While this position was a prestigious one, it could also be very onerous and expensive. In the administrative structure of the late Roman Empire, the decurion was responsible for paying for public entertainment, the maintenance of public works and, most significantly, the collection of taxes from those who lived in the area covered by the council. If there was a shortfall in the amount collected, the difference came out of his own pocket. Some town councillors consequently sought to avoid this and the other expenses by acquiring the one position in the later empire that offered a tax-free status, namely, that of an ordained deacon or presbyter.

When Constantine I had converted to Christianity in the first quarter of the fourth century, he had enthusiastically granted the clergy freedom from taxation. But when this freedom began to be abused, legislation was passed that required those who wished to be ordained to hand over two-thirds of their property to either their sons or relatives. Such legislation would obviously test the sincerity of a person's desire to be ordained.[33]

The fact that Calpornius had managed to hang on to his estate says much about his probable reasons for becoming a deacon. And it provides a background to Patrick's statement that before his captivity in Ireland he "did not know the true God." In the words of Ludwig Bieler, his home was "worldly in spirit, though Christian in name."[34]

---

[29] Jer. 9:16.

[30] Acts 13:47.

[31] *Confession* 1, in *The Works of St. Patrick, St. Secundinus: Hymn on St. Patrick*, trans. Ludwig Bieler (1953; repr., New York: Paulist, nd), 21, altered. This translation, hereafter Bieler, *Works of St. Patrick*, can be found online at various sites.

[32] *Letter to the Soldiers of Coroticus* 10, in Bieler, *Works of St. Patrick*, 43.

[33] This discussion of the role of the decurion in the late Roman Empire is dependent on Hanson, *Saint Patrick: His Origins and Career*, 116–18, 176–79; Hanson, *Historical Saint Patrick*, 22–23; Thompson, *Who Was Saint Patrick?*, 8–9. See also Freeman, *St. Patrick of Ireland*, 2–3.

[34] "St. Patrick and the British Church," in *Christianity in Britain, 300–700*, ed. M. W. Barley and R. C. Hanson (Leicester: Leicester University Press, 1968), 123. See also Christopher Bamford, "The Heritage

The text cited above also gives some indication of the general where-abouts of Patrick's home: the village Bannavem Taburniae, or, as E. A. Thompson and Máire B. de Paor spell it, Bannaventa Berniae.[35] Unfor-tunately, this village has not been identified. Thompson has noted that "Romano-British village names which can be located on the map are few and far between."[36] Nevertheless, it is most probable that this village was near the western coast of Britain, where it would be within easy striking distance of Irish raiders. Most Patrician scholarship has tended to place the village in the south of England, although Alan Macquarrie has recently argued that there is "nothing in the evidence which would be inconsistent with Patrick being a native of north Britain, even of areas like Galloway or Strathclyde north of Hadrian's Wall."[37] Be this as it may, the mention of his father's villa (villulam), which was near this village provides solid evidence that Patrick was born into the upper crust of Romano-British society, and was accustomed to wealth and comfort.[38]

Finally, Patrick's description of himself as "most unlearned" (rusticissimus) is significant. A number of times in his Confession Patrick bemoans the fact that his education was deficient. For instance, in Confession 9 he admits:

> I have not studied like the others, who thoroughly imbibed law and Sacred Scripture, and never had to change from the language of their childhood days, but were able to make it still more perfect. In our case, what I had to say had to be translated into a tongue foreign to me, as can be easily proved from the savour of my writing, which betrays how little instruction and training I have had in the art of words.[39]

While Patrick's contemporaries were becoming progressively skillful in their use of Latin as a literary tool, he was a slave in Ireland, having to speak the language of his captors, Old Irish. His education in Latin had been severely

---

of Celtic Christianity: Ecology and Holiness," in The Celtic Consciousness, ed. Robert O'Driscoll (Toronto: McClelland and Stewart; Dublin: Dolmen, 1981), 172.

[35] Thompson, Who Was Saint Patrick?, 9; de Paor, Patrick: The Pilgrim Apostle of Ireland, 25–26.

[36] Thompson, Who Was Saint Patrick?, 9. In his recent history of Ireland, Thomas Bartlett has stated that he thinks Bannavem Taburniae is "possibly present-day Carlisle on the Anglos-Scottish border." Ireland: A History (Cambridge: Cambridge University Press, 2010), 4.

[37] The Saints of Scotland: Essays in Scottish Church History AD 450–1093 (Edinburgh: John Donald, 1997), 37–41. Gwyn Davies, A Light in the Land: Christianity in Wales 200–2000 (Bridgend, Wales: Bryntirion, 2001), 20, suggests that Patrick may have come from what is today Wales.

[38] See also his statement in the Letter to the Soldiers of Coroticus 10 about giving away his aristocratic status.

[39] Bieler, Works of St. Patrick, 23. See also Confession 10, 12, 13, 46, 62; Letter to the Soldiers of Coroticus 1.

curtailed, and when, much later in life, he came to write the *Confession*, he often struggled to express himself clearly.[40]

So, at the age of sixteen Patrick found himself violently torn away from all that was familiar to him and transported as a slave to the west coast of Ireland. As a result of this intensely traumatic experience, Patrick turned to God. In his own words, "And there [in Ireland] the Lord opened the sense of my unbelief that I might at last remember my sins and be converted with all my heart to the Lord my God, who had regard for my abjection, and mercy on my youth and ignorance."[41]

Patrick went on to recall one thing in particular about the years that followed while he was a captive in Ireland: his attempt to live a life in daily communion with God.

> After I came to Ireland—every day I had to tend sheep, and many times a day I prayed—the love of God and his fear came to me more and more, and my faith was strengthened. And my spirit was moved so that in a single day I would say as many as a hundred prayers, and almost as many in the night, and this even when I was staying in the woods and on the mountain; and I used to get up for prayer before daylight, through snow, through frost, through rain, and I felt no harm, and there was no sloth in me—as I now see, because the Spirit within me was then fervent.[42]

It would appear that Patrick was held captive in what today would be the northwest of Ireland, for he notes that he was not far from the "Western Sea," that is, the Atlantic.[43] After six years of captivity, Patrick managed to escape and eventually find his way back to his family in Britain. The period that elapsed between his return to Britain and his going back to Ireland as a missionary is quite obscure. We do know that in this period Patrick had a striking dream in which he sensed a call to return to Ireland to work among the people who had enslaved him.[44] It was also during this time that he may

---

[40]On Patrick's Latin, see Ludwig Bieler, "The Place of Saint Patrick in Latin Language and Literature," *Vigiliae Christianae* 6 (1952): 65–97; Christine Mohrmann, *The Latin of Saint Patrick* (Dublin: Dublin Institute for Advanced Studies, 1961); Hanson, *Saint Patrick: His Origins and Career*, 158–70; Hanson and Blanc, *Saint Patrick*, 155–63.

[41]*Confession* 2, in Bieler, *Works of St. Patrick*, 21.

[42]*Confession* 16, in Bieler, *Works of St. Patrick*, 25. On the contrast of Christian prayer as found in this description of Patrick's piety with that of both Roman and Celtic paganism, see Freeman, *St. Patrick of Ireland*, 29–30.

[43]*Confession* 23.

[44]*Confession* 23–24.

have received some formal theological training in preparation for ordination as a deacon. Patrick may have gone to Gaul for this training, but there is no indication that he personally visited any other part of the empire or that he was commissioned by the church in Rome.[45] In the course of this preparation, he became thoroughly familiar with the Latin Bible, so much so that Christine Mohrmann has described Patrick as "a man *unius libri*" ("a man of one book").[46]

At the end of this period, that is, around 432, he departed for the part of Ireland where he had been held captive. He would never return to Britain. As he wrote in his *Confession* 43:

> Wherefore, then, even if I wished to leave … and go to Britain—and how I would have loved to go to my country and my parents, and also to Gaul in order to visit the brethren and to see the face of the saints of my Lord! God knows it that I much desired it; but I am bound by the Spirit,[47] who gives evidence against me if I do this, telling me that I shall be guilty; and I am afraid of losing the labour which I have begun—nay, not I, but Christ the Lord who bade me come here and stay with them for the rest of my life, if the Lord will.[48]

And in another text from this same work he could state:

> I came to the people of Ireland to preach the Gospel, and to suffer insult from the unbelievers, bearing the reproach of my going abroad, and many persecutions even unto bonds, and to give my free birth for the benefit of others; and, should I be worthy, I am prepared to give even my life without hesitation and most gladly for his name, and it is there that I wish to spend it until I die, if the Lord would grant it to me.[49]

These texts reveal a man who has a deep certainty of the will of God for his life: to live out his days in Ireland so that the Irish might come to know God as he had done. In the first text he says that he must do this because he is "bound by the Spirit." This phrase, "bound by the Spirit" is drawn directly from Acts 20:22, where the apostle Paul tells the Ephesian elders that he is

---

[45] Pace McKay, Hill, and Buckler, *History of Western Society*, 201.
[46] Mohrmann, *Latin of Saint Patrick*, 8. On Patrick's devotion to the Scriptures, see Hanson, *Historical Saint Patrick*, 44–47.
[47] Cf. Acts 20:22.
[48] *Confession* 43, in Bieler, *Works of St. Patrick*, 35.
[49] *Confession* 37, in Bieler, *Works of St. Patrick*, 32.

"constrained by the Spirit" to go to Jerusalem, despite the probability that he would experience much suffering there. The apostle Paul is committed to doing what he perceives as God's will, no matter the cost. The clear implication in Patrick's use of this term is that he shares the apostle Paul's attitude and depth of commitment.

It needs to be noted that Patrick's writings display the conviction that his evangelistic activity was to be one of the final events of history. He writes:

> I must accept with equanimity whatever befalls me, be it good or evil, and always give thanks to God, who taught me to trust in him always without hesitation, and who must have heard my prayer so that I, however ignorant I was, in the last days dared to undertake such a holy and wonderful work— thus imitating somehow those who, as the Lord once foretold, would preach his Gospel "for a testimony to all nations before the end of the world."[50] So we have seen it, and so it has been fulfilled: indeed, we are witnesses that the Gospel has been preached unto those parts beyond which there lives nobody.[51]

This text dovetails well with the experience of one for whom the disintegration of Roman imperial might was a living reality and who, like other Christians of the day, regarded that event as a sign of the end of the world.[52] It also fits well with one who had been raised with the typical Roman perspective that beyond the shores of Ireland there was only ocean. As R. P. C. Hanson puts it, "To a man of classical antiquity, [Ireland] was literally the last country on earth. It was the most westerly country in Europe; beyond it was nothing."[53] In Patrick's mind, he had been given the incredible privilege of preaching Christianity to literally the last nation to be evangelized.[54]

The course of his travels in Ireland is not at all clear from his *Confession*, but it was probably restricted to the northern half of the island.[55] In human terms, his ministry was extremely successful, though he certainly had not evangelized the whole of the north of Ireland by the time of his death, which

---

[50]See Matt. 24:14.

[51]*Confession* 34, in Bieler, *Works of St. Patrick*, 32.

[52]Thus Hanson, *Saint Patrick: His Origins and Career*, 184–85, 201; Leslie Hardinge, *The Celtic Church in Britain* (London: S.C.K., 1972), 71–72; John T. McNeill, *The Celtic Churches: A History A.D. 200 to 1200* (Chicago: University of Chicago Press, 1974), 59. Pace Bieler, *Works of St. Patrick*, 87n81.

[53]Hanson, *Historical Saint Patrick*, 23.

[54]Freeman, *St. Patrick of Ireland*, 119–25.

[55]Macquarrie, *Saints of Scotland*, 40–41.

cannot have been long after he wrote his *Confession*. As he states near the close of his *Confession*, "This is my confession before I die."[56]

His final days, though, were ones of trouble. As shall be seen, there were those who had opposed his mission to Ireland. Despite the evident success of Patrick's ministry, this opposition did not go away, but appears to have become more vocal with the passing of years. They especially charged him with having undertaken the mission to Ireland for the basest of reasons, namely, financial gain. Patrick's *Confession* was written to lay these criticisms and charges to rest once and for all.[57]

A Missionary Passion

After Patrick's death in the 460s total silence reigns about him in the Irish Christian tradition until the 630s, when he is mentioned by Cummian (d. ca. 661/662), abbot of Durrow. In a letter to Segene, abbot of Iona, Cummian describes Patrick as the "holy Patrick, our father."[58] But the shroud of silence until Cummian's letter should not be taken to mean that Patrick was forgotten. His works, the *Confession* and the *Letter to the Soldiers of Coroticus*, were obviously cherished, copied, and transmitted. Moreover, his missionary labors firmly planted the Christian faith in Irish soil and left a deep imprint on the Celtic church that would grow up from this soil.

Patrick speaks of "thousands" converted through his ministry,[59] including sons and daughters of Irish kings.[60] They were converted, he tells us, from the worship of "idols and filthy things."[61] It is noteworthy that he here speaks of the worship practices of Celtic paganism with "scorn and dislike."[62] In order to increase the range of his influence he ordained "clergy everywhere."[63] Patrick never lost sight of the fact, though, that it was God's grace that lay behind each and every success of his mission. "For I am very much God's debtor," he joyfully confessed, "who gave me such great grace that many people were reborn in God through me."[64]

---

[56] *Confession* 62, in Bieler, *Works of St. Patrick*, 40. See also Thompson, *Who Was Saint Patrick?*, 84–85.

[57] Thompson, *Who Was Saint Patrick?*, 144–46; de Paor, *Patrick: The Pilgrim Apostle of Ireland*, 145–52; Freeman, *St. Patrick of Ireland*, 142–49.

[58] Cited by Hanson, *Saint Patrick: His Origins and Career*, 66.

[59] *Confession* 14, 50; see also *Confession* 38; *Letter to the Soldiers of Coroticus* 2.

[60] *Confession* 41–42.

[61] *Confession* 41.

[62] Hanson, *Historical Saint Patrick*, 111.

[63] *Confession* 38, 40, 50.

[64] *Confession* 38, in Bieler, *Works of St. Patrick*, 32.

Yet, his missionary labors were not without strong opposition, presumably from pagan forces in Ireland. In one section of his *Confession* he says, "Daily I expect murder, fraud, or captivity."[65] He mentions two distinct occasions of captivity, one for two months and the other for a fortnight.[66] He also relates that he was in peril of death "twelve" times, though he gives no details of these lest he bore the reader![67] Patrick's response to these dangers reveals the true mettle of the man: "I fear none of these things because of the promises of heaven. I have cast myself into the hands of God Almighty, who rules everywhere, as the prophet says: 'Cast thy thought upon God, and he shall sustain thee.'"[68]

There was not only external opposition, though. Many of Patrick's Christian contemporaries in the Western Roman Empire appear to have given little thought to evangelizing their barbarian neighbors. As Máire B. de Paor notes, "There was seemingly no organised, concerted effort made to go out and convert pagans, beyond the confines of the Western Roman Empire" during the twilight years of Roman rule in the West.[69] Whatever the reasons for this lack of missionary effort, Patrick's mission to Ireland stands in splendid isolation. As Thompson notes, what we find in the *Confession* is paragraph after paragraph on this issue, bespeaking Patrick's uniqueness in his day.[70]

Thus, when Patrick announced his intention in Britain to undertake a mission to the Irish, there were those who strongly opposed him. "Many tried to prevent this my mission," Patrick recalled. "They would even talk to each other behind my back and say: 'Why does this fellow throw himself into danger among enemies who have no knowledge of God?'"[71] Patrick, though, was assured of the rightness of his missionary activity in Ireland. He knew that he was personally called to evangelize Ireland.[72] He also had a deep sense of gratitude to God for what God had done for him. "I cannot be silent," he declared, "about the great benefits and the great grace which the Lord has deigned to bestow upon me in the land of my captivity; for this we can give to God in return after having been chastened by him, to

---

[65] *Confession* 55, in Bieler, *Works of St. Patrick*, 38.

[66] *Confession* 21, 52.

[67] *Confession* 35.

[68] *Confession* 55, in Bieler, *Works of St. Patrick*, 38.

[69] *Patrick: The Pilgrim Apostle of Ireland*, 23–24.

[70] Thompson, *Who Was Saint Patrick?*, 82–83.

[71] *Confession* 46, in Bieler, *Works of St. Patrick*, 36.

[72] See *Confession* 23.

exalt and praise his wonders before every nation that is anywhere under the heaven."[73]

Most importantly Patrick had a detailed understanding of what the Scriptures clearly teach regarding mission.

> We ought to fish well and diligently, as the Lord exhorts in advance and teaches, saying: "Come after me, and I will make you fishers of men."[74] And again he says through the prophets: "Behold, I send many fishers and hunters, says God," and so on.[75] Hence it was most necessary to spread our nets so that a great multitude and throng might be caught for God, and that there be clerics everywhere to baptize and exhort a people in need and want, as the Lord in the Gospel states, exhorts and teaches, saying: "Going therefore now, teach all nations, baptizing them in the name of the Father, and the Son, and the Holy Spirit, teaching them to observe all things, whatever I have commanded you: and behold I am with you all days even to the consummation of the world."[76] And again he says: "Go therefore into the whole world, and preach the Gospel to every creature. He that believes and is baptized shall be saved; but he that believes not shall be condemned."[77] And again: "This Gospel of the kingdom shall be preached in the whole world for a testimony to all nations, and then the end shall come."[78] And so too the Lord announces through the prophet, and says: "And it shall come to pass, in the last days, says the Lord, I will pour out of my Spirit upon all flesh; and your sons and your daughters shall prophesy, and your young men shall see visions, and your old men shall dream dreams. And upon my servants indeed, and upon my handmaids will I pour out in those days of my Spirit, and they shall prophesy."[79] And in Hosea, he says: "I will call that which was not my people, my people; and her that had not obtained mercy, one that has obtained mercy. And it shall be in the place where it was said: 'You are not my people,' there they shall be called the sons of the living God."[80]

---

[73] *Confession* 3, in Bieler, *Works of St. Patrick*, 21–22.
[74] Matt. 4:19.
[75] Jer. 16:16.
[76] Matt. 28:19–20.
[77] Mark 16:15–16.
[78] Matt. 24:14.
[79] Acts 2:17–28, citing Joel 2:28–29.
[80] *Confession* 40, in Bieler, *Works of St. Patrick*, 33–34, altered. The final quote is from Rom. 9:25–26, citing Hos. 1:10; 2:1, 23.

Finally, we need to note that it was faith in the triune God that had ultimately led Patrick back to Ireland and kept him there. It was for this faith
that he was "bound in the Spirit." It was this faith that he longed to pass on
to the Irish. As he wrote in *Confession* 14, tying faith in the Trinity and mission together:

> In the light, therefore, of our faith in the Trinity I must make this choice,
> regardless of danger I must make known the gift of God and everlasting
> consolation, without fear and frankly I must spread everywhere the name
> of God so that after my decease I may leave a bequest to my brethren and
> sons whom I have baptized in the Lord—so many thousands of people.[81]

The Celtic Church

The Celtic church would inherit Patrick's missionary zeal. His spiritual
descendants, men like Columba (ca. 521–597), Columbanus (ca. 543–615),
and Aidan (d. 651), drank deeply from the well of Patrick's missionary fervor
so that the Celtic church became, in the words of James Carney, "a reser-
voir of spiritual vigor, which would . . . fructify the parched lands of western
Europe."[82] As Diarmuid Ó Laoghaire notes, it is surely no coincidence that
what was prominent in Patrick's life was reproduced in the lives of his heirs.[83]
Throughout the sixth and seventh centuries, Celtic Christians evangelized
the British Isles, Gaul, and central Europe with a passion that matched that
of Patrick, the founder of this group of churches.

Patrick's Celtic Christian heirs also inherited his rich Trinitarian spirituality, which, unlike his missionary passion, was central to Latin Christianity
in late antiquity. Near the very beginning of the *Confession* Patrick sets out
in summary form the essence of his faith in God.

> There is no other God, nor ever was, nor will be, than God the Father
> unbegotten, without beginning, from whom is all beginning, the Lord
> of the universe, as we have been taught; and his son Jesus Christ, whom
> we declare to have always been with the Father, spiritually and ineffably
> begotten by the Father before the beginning of the world, before all begin-
> ning; and by him are made all things visible and invisible. He was made
> man, and, having defeated death, was received into heaven by the Father;

---

[81] *Confession* 14, in Bieler, *Works of St. Patrick*, 24.
[82] "Sedulius Scottus," in *Old Ireland*, ed. Robert McNally (New York: Fordham University Press,
1965), 230.
[83] "Old Ireland and Her Spirituality" in McNally, *Old Ireland*, 33.

"and he hath given him all power over all names in heaven, on earth, and under the earth, and every tongue shall, confess to him that Jesus Christ is Lord and God,"[84] in whom we believe, and whose advent we expect soon to be, "judge of the living and of the dead,"[85] who will render to every man according to his deeds; and "he has poured forth upon you abundantly the Holy Spirit,"[86] "the gift" and "pledge"[87] of immortality, who makes those who believe and obey "sons of God . . . and joint heirs with Christ";[88] and him do we confess and adore, one God in the Trinity of the Holy Name.[89]

An Old Irish prayer, *The Breastplate of Patrick*, though most likely written in the century following Patrick's death, is an excellent example of the way in which Patrick's Trinitarian faith was transmitted. In its opening and closing refrain, it declares:

I rise today
    with a mighty power, calling on the Trinity,
    with a belief in the threeness,
    with a faith in the oneness
    of the Creator of creation.[90]

The creedal statement cited above is the only place in the *Confession* where we can be sure that Patrick is referring to another work besides his Latin Bible. The Latin of the first half of this creed has the "balance and cadences of what passed for polished style in late antiquity" and is clearly not of Patrick's own composition. And although the second half of the creed is filled with biblical quotation or allusion, it too has regular cadences.[91] It is most likely that Patrick is reproducing here a rule of faith used in the British church to instruct new believers about the essentials of the Christian faith.[92]

Hanson, though, has probed further into the source of Patrick's creed and has cogently argued that it essentially stems from one found in the writings

---

[84]Phil. 2:9–11.
[85]Acts 10:42.
[86]Titus 3:5.
[87]Cf. Acts 2:38; Eph. 1:14.
[88]Rom. 8:16–17.
[89]*Confession* 4, in Bieler, *Works of St. Patrick*, 22.
[90]Trans. Freeman, *St. Patrick of Ireland*, 161, 164.
[91]D. R. Bradley, "The Doctrinal Formula of Patrick," *The Journal of Theological Studies*, ns, 33 (1982): 124–33.
[92]Hanson, *Historical Saint Patrick*, 79, 81; Bradley, "Doctrinal Formula of Patrick," 133.

of Victorinus of Pettau (d. 304), who died as a martyr in the Diocletianic persecution. Certain additions have been made to Victorinus's creed in light of the Trinitarian controversies of the fourth century.[93]

The mention above of Patrick's bibliocentrism brings us to a final aspect of Patrick's bequest to the Celtic church in Ireland. His Christianity is "very much a religion of the book," namely the Latin Bible.[94] Given the central place that the Bible held in his thinking, it is not surprising that the success of Patrick's mission helped initiate an impetus among the Irish toward literacy. In fact, so profound was this impetus that by the seventh century the Irish had become major participants in one of the key aspects of the Christian *romanitas* (Roman Christianity) of late antiquity: "bibliocentric literacy."[95]

Such are some of the key aspects of the long-range legacy of the mission of Patrick, who had simply come to Ireland to pass on his faith in the "One God in the Trinity of the Holy Name" to the Irish. His *Confession* reveals a transparent personality: a zealous evangelist and loving pastor who was willing to be a stranger in Ireland not his own that Irish men and women might come to know the Savior. It is noteworthy that Patrick "put first in his thought and teaching the great central message of God's love, God's act of redemption in Christ, the call to men to respond to this in faith and love, and the presence of the Spirit in the Church now making that love and redemption a reality for those who believe and obey."[96]

---

[93]"Witness for St. Patrick to the Creed of 381," *Analecta Bollandiana* 101 (1983): 297–99.

[94]Joseph F. T. Kelly, "Christianity and the Latin Tradition in Early Mediaeval Ireland," *Bulletin of the John Rylands University Library of Manchester* 68, no. 2 (Spring 1986): 411; Hanson, *Historical Saint Patrick*, 44–47.

[95]Kelly, "Christianity and the Latin Tradition," 417.

[96]Hanson, *Saint Patrick: His Origins and Career*, 203.

Chapter 8

WALKING WITH THE CHURCH FATHERS

My First Steps on a Lifelong Journey

First Encounter

Like other first-year divinity students I first encountered the church fathers through a survey course on church history. The course was offered in the first year of my studies at Wycliffe College, the University of Toronto. Because Wycliffe College was a part of the Toronto School of Theology (TST), all of the first-year students of the member colleges of TST took the survey course. Our textbook for the section dealing with the ancient church was Henry Chadwick's solid work, *The Early Church* (1967). This was my first real exposure to the Fathers, and I could not have had a better guide. This, along with a delightful experience in learning first-year Greek, laid the foundation for what would prove to be a consuming interest in Patristics.

My first in-depth encounter with the Fathers came through a paper assigned to me by Dr. Jakób Jocz (1906–1983) in the spring of 1975. I was halfway through my first year of the master of religion program, and as a young Christian less than a year in the faith, I was somewhat in awe of Dr. Jocz, a third-generation Hebrew Christian from Lithuania who was a profound scholar and a man who knew his God. When he asked me to examine Novatian's *On the Trinity* and its relationship to the Bible and Greek philosophy—he knew of my background in philosophy—who was I to argue?

I knew nothing about the third-century schismatic or his Trinitarian study, but from that point on I was hooked on the Fathers.

Finding a Mentor in the Fathers: John Egan, S.J.

In my second year I took my first course in Patristics. It was taught by Dr. John Egan, S.J. (1932–1999), one of the most knowledgeable students of the ancient church I have ever known, who soon became my mentor in the Fathers. Of Irish descent, John had entered the Society of Jesus when he was eighteen and subsequently studied classical literature and philosophy at St. Louis University. It was this study in the classics that gave him a superb grasp of the linguistic nuances of both Greek and Latin. After a period of study in Rome, he went on to the Institut Catholique de Paris where he completed his doctoral thesis in 1971 on "The Knowledge and Vision of God According to Gregory Nazianzen: A Study of the Images of Mirror and Light," under Dr. Charles Kannengiesser, an expert in Athanasius and Patristic exegesis, at the Sorbonne in Paris. This doctoral interest in the writings of Nazianzen—or, as John was wont to refer to him, Greg Naz.—proved to be the start of a lifelong fascination with this particular Christian author. Not that John did not have a good grasp of the other major figures in the Greek Patristic tradition or that he could not write on them, but the theological thought of the sermons and poems of Gregory became his special area of study.

Throughout the 1980s and 1990s he gave a goodly number of papers on Nazianzen's theology at conferences held by the Canadian Society of Patristic Studies and the North American Patristics Society, as well as at the Oxford Patristics Conferences. Two areas, in particular, occupied John's attention: Nazianzen's reflections on the meaning of the cross and his Trinitarian thought. In his probing of Nazianzen's exegesis of Psalm 21:2 (LXX), Christ's cry of abandonment, John was not afraid to point out certain inadequacies in Nazianzen's treatment of the humanity of Christ. A number of papers also dealt with this Greek author's use of various ways of describing Christ's death at different periods in his career: the "ransom theory," the so-called deceit of the Devil, the idea of the cross as an atoning sacrifice, and the Christus Victor motif.[1]

---

[1] See, for example, "Gregory Nazianzen's Exegesis of Psalm 21.2 (LXX) in his *Oration* 30.5: Some Recent Value Judgments" (unpublished paper); "The Deceit of the Devil according to Gregory Nazianzen," *Studia Patristica*, ed. Elizabeth A. Livingstone (Louvain: Peeters, 1989), 22:8–13.

John's study of Nazianzen's Trinitarian thought and the language clothing that thought produced a series of fascinating papers.[2] A couple of these
papers, dealing with the imagery of light, developed ideas that clearly had their
roots in John's thesis. Three papers centered on a major issue for Patristic
Trinitarianism: how can the Father be considered the "primal cause" of the
other two members of the Godhead and yet the essential and eternal equal-
ity of the three members of the Godhead be maintained? John believed that
Nazianzen was able to balance both of these ideas since, for Gregory, both
"origination and reciprocal relations are the dynamic order which constitute
the Trinity."

John's delight in the Fathers was deeply rooted in the fact that the thinking
of these early giants of the Christian church was central to his own faith. In
particular, I suspect that John's love for the writings of Nazianzen was in part
linked to the fact that they helped point John to the One of whom Nazianzen
never tired of speaking, namely, the triune God.

I will ever thank God that I had the enormous privilege of having this
gifted man serve as my early mentor in the study of the church fathers. The
course I took from him in 1976 was on the knowledge of God in the third- and
fourth-century Greek and Latin fathers. John's focus on the primary sources
and rigorous methods of study opened up the vast riches of Patristic literature.
Further courses with John followed: in Patristic theological anthropology, in
the christology of the Fathers, and reading courses in Clement of Alexandria,
Origen, and his favorite theologian, Gregory of Nazianzus.

Other Encounters with the Fathers

Through these years of my master's degree I took every opportunity to dive
into the Fathers. For example, when my mother, Teresa V. Haykin (1933–
1976), died, I decided to write a paper on Irenaeus's concept of the beatific
vision for a course taught by Eugene R. Fairweather (1921–2002), then of
Trinity College. Professor Fairweather was a remarkable man, a polymath in
many ways, and a delight to listen to as a lecturer. He had distinct eccentrici-
ties, though, one of which was a habit of not returning students' papers and

---

[2]See, for example, "Towards a Mysticism of Light in Gregory Nazianzen's *Oration* 32.15," in *Studia
Patristica*, ed. Elizabeth A. Livingstone (Louvain: Peeters, 1989), 28/3:473–81; "Primal Cause and
Trinitarian Perichoresis in Gregory Nazianzen's *Oration* 31.14," in *Studia Patristica*, ed. Elizabeth A.
Livingstone (Louvain: Peeters, 1993), 27:21–28; "Toward Trinitarian *Perichoresis*: Saint Gregory the
Theologian, *Oration* 31.14," *The Greek Orthodox Theological Review* 39 (1994): 83–93; "αἴτιος/'Author,'
αἰτία/'Cause' and ἀρχή/'Origin': Synonyms in Selected Texts of Gregory Nazianzen," in *Studia Patristica*,
ed. Elizabeth A. Livingstone (Louvain: Peeters, 1997), 32:102–7.

even occasionally not submitting marks for the students in his courses! Happily, though, he returned my paper on Irenaeus and gave me a mark that was duly submitted to the registrar at my home college, Wycliffe. He wrote at the close of my paper, "I hope you plan to do further Patristic studies." No doubt this was an encouragement that helped a little to determine the direction of my future scholarly path. But what mattered most to me at the time was how Irenaeus's biblical view of the future was such a comfort to me following the death of my mother.

Central to Irenaeus's eschatological vision is the fact that the Holy Spirit is "the ladder of ascent to God."[3] The Holy Spirit enables the redeemed to ascend to the vision of God by first

> preparing humanity in the Son of God, the Son then leads humanity to the Father, and the Father bestows incorruption for eternal life, which comes to each one as a result of seeing God. Just as those who see the light are in the light and share in its splendor, so are those who see God: they are in God and share in his splendor. The splendor gives them life; and thus those who see God lay hold of life.[4]

The division between Creator and creature is not violated, but men and women finally realize the purpose of their creation: to glory in God and indeed to be so filled with that glory, they become brilliant reflections of it. This is life indeed.

Then, when I had opportunities to lead morning or evening prayer in the Wycliffe College chapel, the Fathers were frequently helpful. I would often give a small homily based on one of the lectionary readings. When I did so, the Fathers' exegesis of the particular reading I had chosen to speak on might make an appearance. For instance, in a homily on Mark 8:31 that I gave on March 22, 1979, I used a passage from the letter of Clement of Rome (fl. 90–100) to recall the way the early church viewed the apostle Paul as a model of discipleship. A homily on 1 Kings 22:1–28, given in chapel on October 5, 1979, referred to the explanation by Theodoret of Cyrrhus (ca. 393–ca. 457) of this passage, which I felt failed to do justice to the text.

---

[3] *Against the Heresies* 3.24.1, in *The Holy Spirit*, trans. J. Patout Burns and Gerald M. Fagin, Message of the Fathers of the Church 3 (Wilmington, DE: Michael Glazier, 1984), 36.
[4] *Against the Heresies* 4.20.5–6 (my translation).

The Celtic Fathers

When I came to do a doctorate at TST and the University of Toronto in 1977, there was no question about the general area: it would be in church history, and specifically Patristics. In the church history doctoral program at that time the only courses that one needed to take were those that one's thesis committee decided would be helpful in preparation for the comprehensive examinations. I was required to take but one course in addition to language preparation in German and Latin, and that was a course in historiography taught by Cyril Powles (1918–). There was one major paper required in the course, and I elected to do mine on the Venerable Bede (672–735), whom I have generally considered to be the terminus of the Patristic era in the West.[5] I examined Bede's portrayal of Wilfrid of York (ca. 634–ca. 709) in his monumental *Church History*. This coincided with a growing interest in the Celtic church, an interest I have never lost.

To some degree I suppose this interest is traceable to my having been raised in an Irish household. But I also found something pristine in the witness of men such as Patrick, Columba, and Aidan of Lindisfarne. They had a love for the Scriptures and a passion for mission that is truly exemplary. Yet, it needs to be noted that Celtic Christianity is not without its problems. For example, the sort of eremitic asceticism that was associated with the first generations of monks in Egypt and Syria was not uncommon in Ireland and other centers of Celtic Christianity. Thankfully, my doctoral studies were emphasizing the importance of a close reading of primary sources to understand an era. This methodology helped me to avoid the romanticizing of the Celtic church that has taken place in recent years, which has foisted upon believers a variety of modern-day concerns that have few historical roots in the era of the Celtic saints.[6]

Doctoral Studies on Athanasius and Basil

When I began my doctoral studies, TST and the University of Toronto were blessed with a number of remarkable Patristic scholars, including Joanne McWilliam (d. 2008), John M. Rist, and Timothy D. Barnes. Especially influential on my studies was Paul J. Fedwick, who was professor of Patristics at

---

[5] In this I would differ from the view mentioned in chapter 1, that Isidore of Seville marks the close of the Patristic era in the West.

[6] See especially Donald E. Meek, *The Quest for Celtic Christianity* (Edinburgh: Handsel, 2000). See also the overview of Gwyn Davies, *A Light in the Land: Christianity in Wales 200–2000* (Bridgend, Wales: Bryntirion, 2002), 19–27.

St. Michael's College and an expert in Basil of Caesarea. Fedwick's devotion to studying Basil has borne rich fruit in his ten-volume *Bibliotheca Basiliana Universalis* (1993–2010). It was a privilege to have Dr. Fedwick as one of the readers of my thesis when it was completed in 1982.

The main influence on my doctoral studies was, of course, John Egan, my *Doktorvater*. Between the fall of 1979 and the close of 1981 I met weekly with John to discuss my work on the pneumatology of Athanasius and Basil. John taught me how to read their writings with sensitivity and how to develop an eye for the presuppositions that shaped their thought and reflection on Scripture. My thesis sought to discern the way in which Scripture shaped the response of Athanasius and Basil to the Pneumatomachian denial of the deity of the Holy Spirit. I was convinced then, and still am, that Scripture was the central ground of the debates about the Spirit, not politics and not philosophy. But I was also persuaded that the specifics of the Fathers' reading of the Bible in this debate were shaped by the questions they brought to the biblical text. In this I sought to take seriously the fact that in all biblical interpretation there are always two horizons of interpretation: that of the Scriptures and that of the interpreter or exegete.[7] This does not mean that all interpretations are equally valid. It simply recognizes that every act of interpretation is colored right from the very start of the process of exegesis by the questions that are being asked of the text, questions that are determined to some degree by the interpreter's existential situation. If the exegete allows his own context to ask questions that distort the message of the biblical text he or she is interpreting, the biblical text is still there awaiting the interpreter who will ask of it the questions that will yield a truer interpretation.

In the case of the Pneumatomachian controversy I did not, and still do not, believe that either Athanasius or Basil distorted the biblical witness to the Spirit by their questions. The Scriptures are informed by an implicit Trinitarianism that flames out here and there (as in passages like 1 Cor. 12:4–6 and 2 Cor. 13:14). The questioning of Scripture by the two orthodox theologians helped reveal what the church had instinctively known in the centuries of worship and proclamation before the Arian controversy.[8]

---

[7]See Anthony C. Thisleton, *The Two Horizons: New Testament Hermeneutics and Philosophical Description with Special Reference to Heidegger, Bultmann, Gadamer, and Wittgenstein* (Exeter: Paternoster; Grand Rapids: Eerdmans, 1980).

[8]See my *The Spirit of God: The Exegesis of 1 and 2 Corinthians in the Pneumatomachian Controversy of the Fourth Century* (Leiden: E. J. Brill, 1994).

A highlight of my wrestling with the exegesis of Athanasius and Basil was a conference celebrating the sixteenth centenary of the death of Basil. Organized by the Basil expert Paul Fedwick, it was held at the University of St. Michael's College, Toronto, on June 10–16, 1979. Situated near the beginning of my thesis, it had a decisive impact in shaping my thought. Though that was over thirty years ago, the joy and privilege of listening to some of the finest Patristic scholars then alive remains with me. Among those whose presentations are still memorable was that of the monk Jean Gribomont (1920–1986), whose paper, "Notes biographiques sur s. Basile le Grand,"[9] had to be given in the dark since there was a power failure near the beginning of it. Suddenly we were translated back to the days of Basil as he read his paper with the aid of a candle! Then, there was the brilliant study by John Rist of the influence of Neoplatonism on Basil, which turned out to be nearly a hundred pages when printed.[10]

One paper by a renowned German patrologist I also recall as outstanding in both delivery and content: Reinhart Staats's study of the reasons for the acceptance of the Basilian glorification of the Spirit at the Council of Constantinople in the creedal statement that we know as the Nicene Creed. As a fledgling scholar, I was mesmerized by the skill and power of his delivery and argument. Of all the papers at the conference it is probably the one I remember the most to this day. Staats argued that a group of monks whose theological position was akin to that of Macarius-Symeon played an influential role at the council. Macarius-Symeon taught that such is the power of evil in human lives that the only resource capable of overcoming it is the indwelling Holy Spirit. The experiential focus of these monks was, Staats maintained, and I came to agree, a key factor in the formulation of the article on the Holy Spirit at the Council of Constantinople.[11]

A final memorable paper was that delivered by the twentieth-century doyen of Patristic studies, Jaroslav Pelikan (1923–2006).[12] I had read much of Pelikan's work on the Fathers, including his magisterial five-volume *The*

---

[9] *Basil of Caesarea: Christian, Humanist, Ascetic: A Sixteen-Hundredth Anniversary Symposium*, ed. Paul Jonathan Fedwick (Toronto: Pontifical Institute of Mediaeval Studies, 1981), 1:21–48.

[10] "Basil's 'Neoplatonism': Its Background and Nature," in ibid., 1:137–220.

[11] The paper was later printed separately from the other symposium papers as "Die Basilianische Verherrlichung des Heiligen Geistes auf dem Konzil zu Konstantinopel 381. Ein Beitrag zum Ursprung der Formel 'Kerygma und Dogma,'" *Kerygma und Dogma* 25 (1979): 232–53.

[12] For an excellent introduction to Pelikan's life and thought, see Valerie Hotchkiss and Patrick Henry, eds., *Orthodoxy and Western Culture: A Collection of Essays Honoring Jaroslav Pelikan on His Eightieth Birthday* (Crestwood, NY: St Vladimir's Seminary Press, 2005), which contains reflections on his life by Pelikan, as well as a bibliography of his writings.

Christian Tradition: A History of the Development of Doctrine (1971–1989), of which the first volume, dealing with the Fathers, is the single best introduction to Patristic thought.[13] Pelikan's address was a superb talk on the very subject of my thesis, "The 'Spiritual Sense' of Scripture: The Exegetical Basis for St. Basil's Doctrine of the Holy Spirit"[14] and helped orient me in certain aspects of my approach.

My doctoral studies in the Fathers taught me a number of key principles of study when it comes to Patristics. First, there is no substitute for careful reading of the primary sources and that, if possible, in the original languages. Then, interaction with Patristic scholarship is vital, and for this a number of European languages are required, especially German and French and, to a lesser degree, Italian and Spanish. Finally, there needs to be wide reading in the history of the ancient world. Even though the ancient church regarded itself as separate from the world, it is a fundamental mistake to forget the larger social and political context of the Fathers. Like us, they could not escape their times, no matter how hard they tried to spurn the world as martyrs or confessors or to renounce it as monks.

A Lifelong Love

Upon the completion of my doctoral studies, I took up my first teaching position, at Central Baptist Seminary in Toronto, and the Fathers no longer filled the entire frame of my horizon. As the only church historian on faculty, I was expected to lecture on the full gamut of Christianity's history, and getting lectures prepared on other areas of church history took up an enormous amount of time. But even as a person never forgets the first time he or she was smitten by love, so I have never forgotten my love of the Fathers. Time and again over the past twenty-eight years of lecturing I have come back to them to learn theology, to be refreshed spiritually, and to think about what it means to be a Christian. They have truly proven to be a lifelong love.

---

[13] See appendix 2 for my reflections, both positive and critical, on this magisterial volume.
[14] Fedwick, *Basil of Caesarea*, 1:337–60.

Appendix 1

READING THE FATHERS

A Beginner's Guide

Where does one begin reading the Fathers? Well, first of all, I would start with two tremendous secondary sources: Robert Louis Wilken, *The Spirit of Early Christian Thought: Seeking the Face of God* (Yale University Press, 2003) and Henry Chadwick, *The Early Church* (Penguin, 1993). Together these will provide an excellent orientation in terms of the history of the Patristic era (Chadwick) and the spirituality of the Fathers (Wilken). If one is so inclined, Jaroslav Pelikan's *The Christian Tradition: A History of the Development of Doctrine*, vol. 1, *The Emergence of the Catholic Tradition (100–600)* (University of Chicago Press, 1971) is the finest introduction to the thought of the Fathers. While not an easy book, it is a gem.

For a good overview of the period, see the relevant pages in Tim Dowley, ed., *Introduction to the History of Christianity* (Fortress, 1995), and for the key leaders, see the biographies in John D. Woodbridge, ed., *Great Leaders of the Christian Church* (Moody Press, 1988). The latter is regrettably out of print, but secondhand copies can be gotten easily. I have also had published *Defence of the Truth: Contending for the Truth Yesterday and Today* (Evangelical Press, 2004), which deals with theological challenges faced by the ancient church.

Of course, one must not avoid getting into the Fathers directly. Any advice here is bound to be somewhat eclectic, but I would recommend starting with Augustine's *Confessions*, the masterpiece of Patristic piety. Then I would read, not surprisingly, Basil of Caesarea, *On the Holy Spirit*, which, as we have seen, is a masterly combination of fourth-century piety and theology. The second-century *Letter to Diognetus* is an excellent entry point into early Christian apologetics, and *The Odes of Solomon* an overlooked gem of worship, also from the second century. In recent years I have had a renewed interest in the Latin tradition, and here I would recommend Cyprian's *Letter to Donatus* and Hilary's *On the Trinity*, book 1, which recounts the story of his conversion. In the Patristic era many were impacted by Athanasius's *Life of Antony*. Personally I find this work somewhat off-putting even if it is a fascinating window into early monastic thought. I much prefer Gregory of Nyssa's warm account of his sister, *The Life of Macrina*. Finally, Patrick's *Confession* is a must read for reasons enumerated in chapter 7.

Appendix 2

Reflections on Jaroslav Pelikan, *The Emergence of the Catholic Tradition (100–600)*

D oing history has been well likened to the construction of a building. To put up a well-constructed edifice one needs both bricklayers and craftsmen skilled in the details of construction, as well as architects to provide the schematic plans and overall guidance for the project. Similarly in the writing of history we need both the quarrying of primary sources and the detailed work of asking what this event or text means, as well as the overall vision of how a multitude of texts or events fit together. And just as it is rare to find one individual today who does both tasks in the building process—the actual building of the edifice and the drawing up of architectural plans—so it is rare to find historians who excel in both areas. Jaroslav Pelikan, though, is undoubtedly such a rarity.

Pelikan is quite evidently at home with both the details of Patristic scholarship—for example, the critical history of Ignatius of Antioch's letters or the use of Scripture in the fourth-century Pneumatomachian controversy—and the overall sweep of doctrine in this formative period—for instance, the development of christology. His perspective is informed by both rigorous, detailed scholarship and an authoritative grasp of the interconnectedness and main lineaments of Christian doctrine. And all of this is executed while being "passionately convinced of the lasting significance of the patristic achievement."[1] No doubt Pelikan would agree with Adolf von Harnack—whom Pelikan called the "high priest of *Wissenschaft*"[2]—that "the most important period of all [church history] is the early Church—here are the measuring rods for all the rest. . . . Because the decisive questions in Church history are raised in this first period, so the Church historian needs to be at home here above all."[3] Not only is Pelikan in agreement with this view of Harnack, but his five-volume history of Christian doctrine has been written in conscious response to Harnack's *Lehrbuch der Dogmengeschichte* (3 vols., 1886–1889), a work that Pelikan notes has been "superseded but never surpassed, . . . the one interpretation of early Christian doctrine with which every other scholar in the field must contend."[4]

One of the great themes of Harnack's work is that the deep-seated Patristic interest in dogma is actually an alien imposition of Graeco-Roman patterns of thinking upon Christianity, what he calls "Hellenization."[5] Pelikan responds to Harnack's accusation by emphasizing that Hellenization is not as widespread as Harnack believes. Pelikan cites the theological achievement of Clement of Alexandria and Origen, both of whom have been considered "consistent hellenizer[s]," but whose philosophical categories of thought, upon close examination, are seen to be profoundly modified in light of Scripture.[6] Yet, as he also shows from the work of two very different authors like Tertullian and Gregory of Nyssa, Graeco-Roman thought was very difficult for early Christians to avoid, especially when it came to the nature of the soul and the impassibility of God.[7] In the final analysis, though, it is the various heretical systems opposed by the Fathers that reveal the deepest impress of Hellenization. In condemning them, the church was seeking to protect Christian doctrine from the encroachment of secular thought.[8]

---

[1] Henry Chadwick, "Book Notes: Pelikan, Jaroslav: *The Christian Tradition: A History of the Development of Christian [sic] Doctrine. Vol. I: The Emergence of the Catholic Tradition," The Journal of Religion* 54 (1974): 315.

[2] *The Melody of Theology: A Philosophical Dictionary* (Cambridge, MA: Harvard University Press, 1988), 111. For an overview of the life and thought of Harnack, see William H. C. Frend, *From Dogma to History: How Our Understanding of the Early Church Developed* (London: SCM, 2003), 9–31.

[3] Letter to Karl Holl, 1859, cited by B. Drewery, "History and Doctrine: Heresy and Schism," *Journal of Ecclesiastical History* 23 (1972): 251–52.

[4] *The Christian Tradition: A History of the Development of Doctrine*, vol. 1, *The Emergence of the Catholic Tradition (100–600)* (Chicago: University of Chicago Press, 1971), 359.

[5] See ibid., 45, 55.

[6] Ibid., 46–55.

[7] Ibid., 49–54.

[8] Ibid., 55.

Moreover, what is often considered the supreme symbol of Hellenization is the term *homoousios*, used, as is well known, by the Council of Nicaea in 325 to describe the ontological relationship between the Father and the Son within the Godhead. Yet, this use of the term actually draws a sharp line between the Christian faith and the philosophical perspective of the surrounding pagan culture of that day, namely Neoplatonism. Whereas third- and fourth-century Neoplatonism postulated "a descending hierarchy of unequal first principles,"[9] the *homoousios* unequivocally affirms the full deity of the Son and leaves absolutely no room for a subordinationist vision of the Godhead. In this respect, the final outcome of the Trinitarian discussion in the fourth century represents a de-Hellenization of dogma and one of the most profound challenges to Graeco-Roman thought in the ancient world.

Personally, I would find myself in broad agreement with Pelikan's answer to what has been a major approach of numerous late nineteenth-century and twentieth-century students of Patristic thought.[10] Nevertheless, there is room to ask if the very concept of the Hellenization of Christianity as enunciated by Harnack, a concept that demands a clear-cut and rigid demarcation between Judaism and Hellenism, is historically accurate?[11] Or is it an explanation that is primarily ideologically motivated? Is it not the case that there was an extensive interpenetration of Jewish and Greek thought before the era of the Fathers, as seen, for instance, in the work of such figures as Aristobulus of Paneas, Philo, and even Josephus? Even in the New Testament one needs to take note of the ease with which the apostle Paul can quote pagan sources in his sermon on the Areopagus and in Titus 1. Are the very sources of the Christian tradition then guilty of Hellenization? Or is it the case that the interplay of thought in the world of the New Testament and the Fathers is somewhat more subtle than the idea of Hellenization allows? What R. M. Price suggests with reference to the ante-Nicene authors may well be correct as a general principle

---

[9] R. M. Price, "'Hellenization' and Logos Doctrine in Justin Martyr," *Vigiliae Christianae* 42 (1988): 21.

[10] It is noteworthy that a key aspect of the current debate about the openness of God has to do with the charge made by the proponents of Open Theism that classical theism has been deeply distorted by Hellenistic thought. See, for example, John Sanders, "Historical Considerations," in *The Openness of God: A Biblical Challenge to the Traditional Understanding of God*, ed. Clark Pinnock (Downers Grove, IL: InterVarsity, 1994), 59–60. More generally Brian D. McLaren has recently maintained that Western Christianity is preaching a gospel that is more shaped by what he calls "the Greco-Roman narrative" than the Scriptures (*A New Kind of Christianity: Ten Questions That Are Transforming the Faith* [New York: HarperCollins, 2010], 33–45). This is simply a new variant of the old charge of Hellenization raised by liberal theologians like Harnack. At best, it is uninformed; at worst, it is irresponsible.

[11] For some of what follows, see Price, "'Hellenization,'" 18–23.

with regard to this whole debate over "Hellenization" and early Christian thought: "Grand vistas of hellenization . . . are a distracting irrelevance that distort the picture and raise the wrong questions. We need to draw a more intricate map of the intellectual world of the pre-Nicene period, with more attention to the subtle and undramatic gradations of the terrain."[12] Pelikan's response to Harnack's thesis of Hellenization could have been strengthened if he had begun his account with the New Testament, thereby showing the strong links between New Testament thought and what followed.[13] Given Pelikan's emphasis on the importance of biblical exegesis for the development of doctrine in the Patristic era, this omission is strange.

Equally strange and startling is the lack of real discussion of Augustine's Trinitarian perspective. Augustine's enormously influential Trinitarianism is summed up and dismissed in one sentence,[14] though Pelikan is certainly aware of its importance in Western Christianity.[15] Elsewhere, Pelikan can actually state that Augustine's *On the Trinity* is, for the Latin West, "the classic summation of the central teaching of Christianity" and may rightly be reckoned as Augustine's "most brilliant intellectual and theological achievement."[16] One wonders if there is more at stake here than simple oversight. For instance, it is noteworthy that Pelikan's treatment of Augustine's defense of the sovereignty of grace in the salvation of sinners is unmistakably critical of the North African theologian.[17] This is curious in light of the clear attempt by Pelikan to present the various heretics of the Patristic era—men like Marcion and Arius[18]—in as sympathetic light as possible.[19] And even more curious when Pelikan later gave it as his opinion that Augustine is "arguably, the only figure from all of late antiquity . . . whom we can still read with understanding and empathy."[20]

---

[12]Ibid., 22.

[13]Robert L. Wilken, "*The Christian Tradition: A History of the Development of Doctrine.* Vol. I: *The Emergence of the Catholic Tradition (100–600),*" *Saturday Review*, August 7, 1971, 26.

[14]*Emergence of the Catholic Tradition*, 224. This omission is also noticed by Chadwick, "The Christian Tradition," 316; Ernest L. Fortin, "Book Reviews: The Christian Tradition: A History of the Development of Doctrine 1: The Emergence of the Catholic Tradition (100–600). By Jaroslav Pelikan," *Theological Studies*, 33 (1972): 331.

[15]*Emergence of the Catholic Tradition*, 67, 197, 350–51.

[16]*Melody of Theology*, 16.

[17]See, for instance, *Emergence of the Catholic Tradition*, 313, 321, 325.

[18]For example, Pelikan can say that Arianism "was more aware of the nuances of the trinitarian problem than its critics were" and that it "helped to keep churchly doctrine both honest and evangelical" (*Emergence of the Catholic Tradition*, 200).

[19]I. John Hesselink, "Book Reviews: Jaroslav Pelikan. *The Emergence of the Catholic Tradition (100–600),*" *Christian Scholar's Review* 2 (1973): 375.

[20]*Melody of Theology*, 17–18.

The omission of Augustine's Trinitarianism is one of a number of notice-able lacunas. Another is an examination of the Apostles' Creed, which is without doubt the most important of Western creedal statements. There are a few brief mentions of it but without any real discussion.[21] The so-called apostolic fathers also receive scant attention, though they are important links between the apostolic era and second-century Christianity.[22] One thinks of Irenaeus of Lyons's link with the apostle John via Polycarp of Smyrna.

These omissions are matched by some odd inclusions. For example, Pelikan notes that among the defenders of the Nicene Creed, obviously Athanasius deserves "pride of place," but, he continues, two other Eastern theologians deserve to be ranged alongside him, namely, "Amphilochius [of Iconium] and especially Didymus."[23] It is certainly curious to see Amphilochius mentioned, who, from a strictly theological perspective, is the least of the Cappadocian fathers and whose written corpus that has come down to us is ever so slight.

But probably my greatest problem with Pelikan's work has to do with his methodology. While it is encouraging to see him include in this study not merely formal theological works but also material drawn from the worship and liturgy of the church, his attempt to treat the church's theology in isolation from the social and personal matrix in which it took shape is deeply regrettable. Pelikan states at the beginning of this study his desire to "listen to the chorus more than to the soloists."[24] But, as he came to admit in the fifth volume in this history of Christian doctrine, there "have been a few soloists . . . whose life and teaching have made them . . . major themes for the chorus, rather than primarily soloists in their own right."[25] From the early church fathers he cites two—Origen and Augustine. If this is the case, then the lives of the theologians who produced the themes for the chorus must be considered.

As R. F. Evans stresses in one of his books on Pelagius:

> The comparison of systems of thought involves an abstraction from the actual course of events. In theological controversies it is not in the first instance systems of thought which "confront" each other, but men—men

---

[21] *Emergence of the Catholic Tradition*, 117, 150–51. For this omission, see Robert L. Calhoun, "A New History of Christian Doctrine: A Review Article," *Journal of the American Academy of Religion* 40 (1972): 503.

[22] See Carl J. Peter, "The Beginnings of Christian Doctrine," *Interpretation* 26 (1972): 224–25.

[23] *Emergence of the Catholic Tradition*, 203.

[24] Ibid., 122.

[25] *The Christian Tradition: A History of the Development of Doctrine*, vol. 5, *Christian Doctrine and Modern Culture (since 1700)* (Chicago: University of Chicago Press, 1989), 7.

who speak and write on concrete occasions, men whose thought may be in flux and may be bent by the very events of controversy in which they are participating.[26]

Moreover, when we remember that the writings of the early church were personal works, directed to specific individuals or to particular groups and caught up in networks of personal relationships, Pelikan's consideration of the doctrine of these works apart from their personal matrix is inevitably problematic.

Consider, for example, Basil of Caesarea's *On the Holy Spirit* (375), the subject of chapter 6, above. It grew out of Basil's controversy with Eustathius of Sebaste, one of his closest friends, indeed the man who had been his mentor when he first became a Christian. As we have seen, Eustathius's interest in the Spirit seems to have been focused on the Spirit's work, not his person. For him, the Holy Spirit was primarily a divine gift within the Spirit-filled person, One who produced holiness. For a number of years, Basil sought to win Eustathius over to a confession of the Spirit's divinity. Despite Eustathius's signing of an orthodox statement in the summer of 373, he eventually broke with Basil and denounced the bishop of Caesarea as being guilty of modalism. And as we saw, this parting of friends eventually led Basil to write one of the most important books of the entire Patristic period, *On the Holy Spirit*. Can the precise form of Basil's pneumatology in this work be genuinely appreciated apart from some awareness of the context that drew it forth?

Or consider Augustine's anti-Pelagian works.[27] His early writings against Pelagianism are basically an exchange of letters with Count Flavius Marcellinus, an imperial official based in Carthage. Marcellinus submitted a list of questions to Augustine, and in response Augustine wrote *On the Merits and Forgiveness of Sins and on the Baptism of Infants* (412). Marcellinus was mystified by one of Augustine's points in this work and asked for a further explanation, which Augustine gave in *On the Spirit and the Letter* (412). Soon after this Augustine began writing *On Nature and Grace* (413–415). It was a reply to Pelagius's *On Nature* and was written specifically to the two individuals who had sent Augustine a copy of Pelagius's work. Toward the close of the Pelagian controversy in the 420s, Augustine wrote the treatises

---

[26]Cited by Drewery, "History and Doctrine: Heresy and Schism," 252.
[27]This paragraph draws on William S. Babcock, "Christian Culture and Christian Tradition in Roman North Africa," in *Schools of Thought in the Christian Tradition*, ed. Patrick Henry (Philadelphia: Fortress, 1984), 34.

On Grace and Free Will and *On Rebuke and Grace* (426–427) as a result of Augustine's correspondence with Valentinus, the abbot of the North African monastery of Hadrumetum, whose monks had raised questions about Augustine's teaching.

Clearly these works by Basil and Augustine do not belong to the category of purely private and personal correspondence. They were intended to have a wider circulation well beyond their initial recipients. But they do show how Patristic writings and Patristic doctrine were frequently embedded in personal contexts. And for that doctrine to be properly understood, it must be seen in the matrix out of which it arose. As Michael Blecker has rightly affirmed, "To do theology without history is to study cut flowers, not living plants."

INDEX